Luftwaffe

The illustrated history of the German Air Force in WWII

Luftwaffe

The illustrated history of the German Air Force in WWII

Dr John Pimlott

AURUM PRESS

**This book is dedicated to the author,
Dr John Pimlott, who died soon after completing it.**

First published in Great Britain 1998
by Aurum Press Ltd, 25 Bedford Avenue, London WC1B 3AT
© Brown Packaging Books Ltd 1998

A catalogue record for this book is available from the British Library.

ISBN 1 85410 544 2

1 2 3 4 5 6 7 8 9 10

1998 1999 2000 2001 2002

Conceived and produced by Brown Packaging Books Ltd,
Bradley's Close, 74-77 White Lion Street, London N1 9PF

Editor: Peter Darman
Design: Jane Felstead

Printed and bound in Spain

Page 1: A Dornier Do 17Z bomber.
*Page 2: A scene which epitomises the Luftwaffe of the early war years:
swarms of Junkers Ju 87 Stuka dive-bombers head towards their target.*

CONTENTS

CHAPTER 1

GROWING PAINS

Defeat in World War I and the subsequent restrictions of the Versailles Treaty meant the Nazis faced a daunting task with regard to creating a modern air force. But deception and determination worked wonders.

Left: Adolf Hitler addresses the Reichstag in 1938. Above him sits Hermann Göring. It was these two men who were responsible for the decisions that led to the expansion of the Luftwaffe.

Above: A jasta *(squadron) of Fokker D.VII single-seat fighters stands ready for inspection as part of the Armistice agreement in November 1918. The D.VII was a formidable machine in its day.*

On 11 November 1918, after four years of costly and fruitless war, Germany had little choice but to accept an Armistice. With French, British and, increasingly, American forces closing in from the west and revolution spreading from the east, it was obvious that the end was near. For their part, the Allies were determined to prevent a German resurgence. The Armistice proposals were harsh, not least in terms of German airpower. According to

Clause IV, Germany was to 'surrender in good condition 1700 fighting and bombing aeroplanes', including all Fokker D.VII fighters and the entire night-bombing fleet. By 12 December 1918, the new republican government in Berlin announced that it had complied, but according to Allied records only a paltry 516 landplanes and 58 seaplanes had been surrendered in all. It was a pattern of duplicity that was soon to become the norm. Despite

Above: Staatssekretär der Luftfahrt *Erhard Milch (centre), photographed with visiting French Air Force officers, 1937. Milch is widely acknowledged to have been the true architect of the Luftwaffe, although his influence waned as he came to be regarded as a rival by Göring. In the end, Erhard Milch's energy and dedication counted for naught.*

Below: *Taken on the same day as the above photograph, this photograph shows French officers being introduced to Dr Ernst Heinkel (the smaller of the two men in civilian clothes) and, behind him, the World War I air 'ace' Ernst Udet, who was awarded the* Pour le Mérite *during the war. Both were influential players in the early years of the Luftwaffe.*

Above: A mechanic works on the wing of a German monoplane trainer, possibly an early Focke-Wulf design. The provision of trainer aircraft to the nascent Luftwaffe in the mid-1930s had to be a production priority in order to fulfil flying crew requirements, and this undoubtedly delayed the introduction of more sophisticated fighters as manufacturers satisfied the need.

Below: An example of Germany's first post-World War I fighter, the Dutch-manufactured Fokker D.XIII. Powered by a licence-built British Napier engine, the D.XIII was the aircraft most widely used at the secret training base at Lipetsk in the Soviet Union, helping to produce pilots and observers for the future, which ironically included the attack on Russia in June 1941.

the official disbandment of the *Luftstreitkrafte* (the German Army's air and air-defence arm) in January 1919, the German forces still had over 9000 aircraft in their inventories and had no intention of sacrificing air capability meekly.

There were a number of ways to circumvent the Armistice terms. As Germany descended into civil unrest, the army raised *Freikorps* (Free Corps) units from among demobilised soldiers to fight the encroaching Communists, and they were given air squadrons to help them. About 35 *Freikorps* squadrons were raised, fielding some 250-300 aircraft between them, and were used to drop leaflets and even bombs on the civilian population within Germany. The threat subsided, but the squadrons were retained, being absorbed into the newly formed *Reichswehr* (the army of the Weimar Republic). At the same time, the government boosted civil aviation, supporting the use of wartime aircraft to carry mail throughout Germany, while many aircraft factories continued to satisfy orders placed with them before the Armistice. It looked as if Clause IV had failed.

The terms of the Versailles Treaty

The situation changed on 28 June 1919 when the German delegation at peace talks in Paris was presented with the terms of the Versailles Treaty and forced to sign. The Allies were now much more insistent: prohibiting all military aircraft manufacture in Germany and giving the government three months in which to hand over all air force equipment. An attempt to disguise air capability by raising squadrons to support the civil police failed, chiefly because the Allies confiscated German civil aircraft until the government complied. Indeed, the 140 civil aircraft permitted to the

Above left: Heinkel He 51A single-seat fighters prepare for take-off, 1935. First flown in the summer of 1933, the He 51 was a robust machine but one that soon proved obsolete, especially when committed to the Spanish Civil War. By 1939, it had been largely relegated to the training role.

Below left: Hermann Göring, the flamboyant head of the Luftwaffe and confidant *of Hitler within the Nazi Party. A World War I air 'ace', Göring had led the famous Richthofen 'circus' in 1918 following the death of the 'Red Baron', and was holder of the* Pour le Mérite *for bravery. However, he proved weak as an air leader in World War II.*

Below: The Luftwaffe begins to take shape, albeit still in civilian garb. This photograph, taken at Berlin-Tempelhof airport in 1936, shows a Junkers Ju 86 airliner in the foreground, with Junkers Ju 52s and a selection of light aircraft parked behind. Both of the Junkers' designs could be converted easily into bombers, and the Ju 52 was widely used in World War II.

Germans soon became the only means of flight within the country, and even they were severely restricted in terms of speed (169kmph/105mph), ceiling (3962m/13,000ft) and range (200km/125 miles). As a result, the air industry virtually ceased to exist, with factories closing and workers made redundant.

Circumventing the treaty

But the Germans did not give up. By 1924 General Hans von Seeckt, Chief of the Army General Staff, had ensured that a rump of air officers was retained in the *Reichswehr* (180 out of the 3800 officers permitted) and had appointed Captain Ernst Brandenburg to head the Air Office of the Ministry of Transport, so creating close links between civil aviation and the armed forces. In addition, official support was given to the new sport of gliding, with many future Luftwaffe 'aces' gaining their first experience of flight through the government-backed *Deutschen Luftfahrt-Verbande.V*, which was set up in 1920.

Of even more significance was the development of military links with Russia. Both Germany and Russia were worried about

the Poles, and both were 'pariah' states which were together-er in response to widespread hatred and distrust. On 16 April 1922, the Treaty of Rapallo normalised relations between Berlin and Moscow. It also created a framework for secret air and military cooperation, based on a Russian need for German technology and a German need for training facilities beyond the gaze of the Allies. Three years later, an agreement was signed to allow the Germans to build an airbase at Lipetsk, 483km (300 miles) to the southwest of Moscow, and Dutch-built Fokker D.XIII fighters were secretly shipped out. By then, the aircraft manufacturing firm of Junkers had set up a factory at Fili, to the south of Moscow,

with the intention of producing its own designs for both the Russians and the Lipetsk base. In the event, the Junkers factory was a failure, but the training of German pilots – both 'Old Eagles' (wartime officers on refresher courses) and 'Young Eagles' (new recruits) – did help to keep alive the spirit of German military aviation. Lipetsk was to remain open until 1933, by which time over 120 pilots had graduated from the base. The emphasis of their training was firmly on close air support to ground units – no bomber pilots were produced at all – but the opportunity was taken to experiment with new equipment and to train ground crews. It was a successful enterprise.

Above: Luftwaffe anti-aircraft gunners show off their skills at a Nazi Party rally in 1935. The weapon is the newly developed 37mm Flugabwehrkanone (Flak) 18, produced in small numbers while awaiting the appearance of the more effective Flak 36.

Left: As the Luftwaffe emerges into the open, priority is given to training the future airmen of the Reich. Here, eager young cadets, now in the uniform of the Luftwaffe, attend a lecture on aerial navigation, essential in the campaigns to come.

Below: Peering through range-finders, Luftwaffe NCOs estimate the speed and altitude of Junkers Ju 52s in a training exercise. Despite the apparent obsolescence of the kit, the gunners are learning skills that will be used within less than four years.

Meanwhile, the Allies had begun to lift some of the restrictions imposed by Versailles, partly as a 'reward' for apparent German compliance and partly as a response to the near collapse of the German economy in the face of swingeing reparations (money paid to the victorious Allies in compensation for the war). This was most apparent in terms of civil aviation, for no moves were made to prevent the creation of a single airline out of the plethora that had emerged since 1918. On 6 January 1926 Lufthansa emerged, initially with a fleet of 162 aircraft. Under Erhard Milch as Operations (later Commercial) Director, the new airline went from strength to strength, opening up fresh routes and carving

Above: An Arado Ar 95 two-seat reconnaissance and torpedo-bomber floatplane. Armed with two machine guns for defence and either a torpedo (as shown) or bombs for attack, the Ar 95 was not a success and few were built.

itself a leading role in Europe. Many Lufthansa pilots would later join the Luftwaffe, while the existence of commercial aviation allowed Milch to place orders with German aircraft manufacturers for more modern airliners, including the tri-motor Junkers Ju 52. The transformation of airliners into bombers or transports for military use did not prove to be very difficult when the need arose.

Organisation of the Luftwaffe

Plans for the recreation of a military air force – a Luftwaffe – were already well advanced by the late 1920s. Working in strict secrecy, staff officers of the *Reichswehr* had been looking forward to the day when the army might be expanded (it had been restricted by Versailles to 100,000 men), and air squadrons were always included. The economic crisis of 1929-30, triggered by the 'Wall Street Crash', put paid to many of the initial ideas, but the basic plan remained. The aim was to create a *Luftstreitkrafte des Neuen Friedensheeres* (Air Corps of the New Peacetime Army), beginning in 1933-34, with a frontline strength of about 150 aircraft and 50 reserves. They would be organised into 22 *staffeln* (squadrons), 13 of them dedicated to reconnaissance, six to fighters and three to bombers. Close support of ground forces was clearly the intention, with the emphasis on providing aerial 'eyes' and fighter protection to those 'eyes', with only a limited capability to drop bombs.

Above: *Arado Ar 68s, the last fighter biplanes to enter Luftwaffe service. The early pattern fuselage cross dates the photograph as 1938, by which time the Ar 68 was obsolete.*

Below: *Focke-Wulf Fw 56* Stösser *fighters, 1936. An agile and clean-lined aircraft, the Fw 56 could be armed with one or two machine guns, and was used in early dive-bombing experiments.*

Moreover, targets for bombing would be chosen specifically to enhance the capability of ground forces, weakening the enemy at the operational and tactical levels rather than going for his cities or domestic industrial base. These plans received official approval on 10 August 1932, five months before Adolf Hitler was appointed Chancellor of the Reich.

Hitler therefore inherited an embryonic air force, but there can be no doubt that his rise to power gave the Luftwaffe a much needed political and financial boost. Within hours of becoming Chancellor in February 1933, the Nazi leader appointed his close colleague Hermann Göring to be *Reichskommissar für die Luftfahrt* (Reich Commissioner for Air), regarding his experiences as a World War I fighter 'ace' as vital to future developments. However, Goring was deeply involved in politics and much of the work on creating the Luftwaffe fell to Milch, transferred from Lufthansa in 1933 to become *Staatssekretär der Luftfahrt* (Secretary of State for Air). He was helped by a vote of 40 million Reichsmarks (about $9.5m in 1933 values) by the Nazi Cabinet to create an air force – the beginning of a financial preference that was to see a steady rise in the amounts of money devoted to the Luftwaffe. By 1936, more than 38 per cent of the German defence budget would be concentrated on air capability.

Erhard Milch's plans

Milch was an experienced businessman, used to managing a large budget. One of his first acts as *Staatssekretär* was to order fighter and bomber aircraft to be produced to boost the ailing aircraft industry and set up production lines. These early designs were

Above: The third prototype (V3) of the Junkers Ju 87, coded D-UKYQ, shows the gull-winged lines that were to become so familiar over the battlegrounds of Europe in World War II. The V3 differed from earlier prototypes in terms of improved tail surfaces and pilot vision, but the basic design is already apparent.

Above right: The fourth prototype (V4) of the Messerschmitt Bf 109 fighter, photographed in 1936. The V4 was the first version of the aircraft to be fitted with an engine-mounted machine gun, hence the rather clipped appearance of the propeller boss.

Below right: A Messerschmitt Bf 110B long-range Zerstörer *(destroyer) fighter in full wartime livery. It was disappointing when committed to battle and was eventually to find a more effective role as a night-fighter.*

only interim – they included the Heinkel He 51 biplane fighter, Ju 52 bomber conversion and, of necessity, large numbers of trainers – but he needed something to show off to the world once the political decision had been made in May 1933 officially to unveil the Luftwaffe. At the time, Milch's plan was to produce a 51-*staffeln* force with a frontline strength of 600 aircraft (rising rapidly to 1000 as industrial processes developed), but he could hardly leave it there. While the factories geared up, he began the process of building modern airbases throughout Germany, replete with radio and visual navigation systems, good communications and meteorological facilities. The 36 'aerodromes' that emerged would prove invaluable once World War II began.

But problems arose. Of crucial importance was the weak state of the German aircraft industry after 14 years of enforced neglect. In 1933, the industry was employing less than 3500 people in eight widely dispersed factories, and although Nazi interest in air capability soon led to expansion (by mid-1936, nearly 125,000 people were employed), the very speed of that expansion undermined its effectiveness. It took time to train aeronautical engineers and craftsmen, let alone to create factories capable of mass production. Although the results looked good on paper, there were limits to what the industry could do. The situation was not helped by Hitler's insistence in September 1933 that the air force should field 2000 aircraft (he recognised the potential value of such a large fleet in frightening the Allies into accepting revisions to the terms of Versailles), nor by poor relations between the men in charge of Luftwaffe affairs. Göring quickly grew to distrust Milch, regarding him as a rival, and although the Chief of the Air Command Office, General Walter Wever, acted as an effective go-between, his death in an air crash in May 1936 left the door open to damaging friction. Although Göring emerged the victor, the friction did little to aid the Luftwaffe's long-term aims.

None of this prevented expansion. While the factories struggled to produce obsolete designs like the He 51, Milch encouraged the development of the next generation of fighting aircraft. Some of these were already on the drawing boards or at prototype stage – as early as July 1932 a requirement had been issued for the building of a high-speed medium bomber, initially to be disguised as an airliner, and this was to produce both the Dornier Do 17 and Heinkel He 111 – but others were brand new.

New aircraft designs

One of the most important was the Messerschmitt Bf 109 fighter, test-flown in September 1935; another was the Junkers Ju 87 'heavy dive-bomber', popularly known as the Stuka (a name derived from the German for 'dive-bomber': *Sturzkampfflugzeug*), which first flew later in the same year. In fact, the emphasis on the Stuka indicated a growing preference among Luftwaffe planners for dive-bombers rather than level-bombers, it being felt that the former were likely to be much more accurate against pinpoint targets such as troop concentrations or communications networks. This was undoubtedly true, and the Stuka would soon be feared throughout Europe, but it did divert resources from the development of the so-called 'Ural Bomber', which was planned for strategic attacks on long-range enemy targets. The Luftwaffe may have placed the emphasis on a doctrine of close air support, interdiction of enemy supply and communication lines and selected targeting of enemy air capability (including aircraft factories), but

as early as 1936 it was apparent that not all aspects could or would be satisfied. Ominously, the Luftwaffe was already a potentially unbalanced force.

This was not apparent to Germany's rivals in Europe, who watched with mounting horror as the Luftwaffe grew in size. On 1 March 1934, Hitler could call on 77 front-line aircraft only (including a mere 27 bombers and 12 fighters), but once the factories had recovered and, equally importantly, conscription had been reintroduced, the Luftwaffe took off in every sense. By 1 August 1935 the fleet had grown to 1833 aircraft (including 833 bombers and 251 fighters); within less than a year it stood at the awesome figure of 2680 (including over 1000 bombers and 700 fighters). This was a powerful deterrent, shown as such on 7 March 1936 when Hitler openly defied the terms of the Versailles Treaty and marched troops (under air cover) into the demilitarised Rhineland. The Allies made no move to stop him; already, after only three years in power, Hitler had created an air force that seemed to threaten the very fabric of modern societies – after all, 1000 bombers would be unstoppable if they were pitched against cities and industrial sites, dropping bombs and gas that would kill or maim countless thousands of people. The fact that Luftwaffe doctrine was specifically proscribing 'terror bombing' was, of course, unknown to outside observers. All they could see were the massed squadrons and their own apparently puny defences. Their fears were soon to be increased as the Luftwaffe showed its teeth, not against them but in a civil war that was about to engulf Spain.

Above left: *The sixth prototype (V6) of the Junkers Ju 88* Schnellbomber, *widely recognised as the forerunner of the production series. Photographed in early 1940, this particular aircraft has uprated engines with four-bladed propellers and a chin-mounted balloon-cable cutter. The idea of a cable-cutter did not last for long.*

Above: *Always aware of propaganda, the Luftwaffe uses biplane fighters to fly in a swastika pattern over a Nazi Party rally in 1938 in a show of force and intimidation. It was images such as this that helped to persuade potential rivals that Germany had a modern, effective air force. In the late 1930s, the images conveyed the truth: by 1937 the Luftwaffe could field 1000 fighters and 700 bombers. In comparison, by the time war broke out in 1939 Britain had fewer than 1700 combat aircraft, and France could only field 550 fighters and 400 bombers.*

Right: *Adolf Hitler takes the salute at a Nazi Party rally in 1935 as his deputy, Rudolf Hess (seated, left) smiles at the camera. Hitler's insistence on a modern Luftwaffe as an instrument of persuasion and deterrence ensured the provision of development funds, but could do little to make up for years of neglect.*

SPAIN – THE TESTING GROUND

The Luftwaffe cut its teeth in the Spanish Civil War, trying out new aerial tactics and new aircraft. By the time the war ended in 1939, the German Air Force contained a cadre of highly skilled and experienced personnel.

Left: The new found confidence of the Luftwaffe is shown in this portrait of a pilot serving in Spain in 1937.

Above: An early model Heinkel He 111 of Kampfgruppe 88 drops its bombs over a Republican target in Spain, 1937.

The Spanish Civil War began in July 1936, when Generals Jose Sanjurjo and Emilio Mola staged a military coup against the newly elected Socialist Government in Madrid. At the same time, General Francisco Franco seized the colony of Spanish Morocco in the name of the coup leaders. Unfortunately, Franco could not move his troops onto the mainland quickly enough to prevent a government backlash. Within days Spain was split, with the rebels (known as Nationalists) holding most of the north as well as Seville and Cadiz, while the government (the Republicans) retained power in Madrid, the south and east, and the Basque region in the north. The scene was set for a bloody confrontation. Both sides sought aid from abroad – the Republicans from fellow

Socialists in the Soviet Union, the Nationalists from the Fascist powers of Germany and Italy. At first, Hitler was wary of seeming too enthusiastic, for fear of an Anglo-French reaction, but when a Lufthansa Ju 52 was seized by the rebels to carry General Luis Orgaz from the Canaries to Tetuen on 20 July, the die was cast. With Sanjurjo already dead (he was killed in an air crash), Mola was desperate for reinforcements; Franco promised to send troops by air but had only six aircraft at his disposal. On 24 July a Nationalist emissary flew to Berlin to plead for help from Hitler, stressing the need to counter growing Soviet influence in Spain. Two days later, Hitler agreed to provide Ju 52s, with fighter escort, to carry troops across the Straits of Gibraltar, avoiding

Republican naval vessels in the vicinity. Milch was to organise the airlift under the codename *Feuerzauben* ('Magic Fire').

The first German airlift

The airlift began on 28 July with two hastily converted Ju 52s, each carrying 35 men per trip, flying from Morocco to Seville. In the first week, these aircraft alone delivered 1207 men to the Nationalist army, to be followed by a further 1282 in the second week. By then, the main Luftwaffe force of nine Ju 52s, six He 51 fighters, 20 *Flak* 30 20mm anti-aircraft guns and more than 100 men had been prepared in Germany, moving by sea to Seville in the first week of August. The airlift – one of the first in history –

Above: A Heinkel He 111B serving with Kampfgruppe 88 *in Spain shows its nose-art. This particular symbol – a stylised 'E', presumably for* Espanna, *formed by means of a 'flying bomb' – denoted the* 3rd Staffel. *The small triangle to the right gives the octane rating of the fuel on board.*

Left: Nationalist troops, loyal to General Franco, wait at an airfield in Spanish Morocco before boarding the two Junkers Ju 52s close by. These are probably the two aircraft provided initially by Hitler to carry Franco's men to the war zone in late July 1936 – the beginning of German involvement.

Below: A Dornier Do 17F-1 high-altitude reconnaissance aircraft, in Spanish Nationalist colours, prepares for take-off.

little choice but to accept the inevitable. Three days later he authorised the use of German personnel in combat missions, allowing Franco to make full use of air support as his forces swept out of Seville to secure parts of Andalusia and threaten Madrid. Toledo fell to the Nationalists on 27 September 1936.

By the autumn of 1936, the Germans had deployed 146 aircraft to Spain and were organising their own formations, soon to

was to continue until 11 October 1936, by which time over 13,900 men and 274 tonnes (270 tons) of equipment had been delivered in a total of 868 aircraft sorties. Without this commitment, it is doubtful if Franco could have intervened on the mainland, leaving Mola isolated and vulnerable to defeat.

Initially, the Luftwaffe was not permitted to carry out combat sorties, but pilots quickly got caught up in the fighting. As early as 13 August, two Ju 52s, converted to bombers, attacked the Republican battleship *Jaime I*; 11 days later German-piloted He 51s escorted Spanish-manned Ju 52s as they carried out a raid against an airbase at Getafe. Indeed, the first fighter air-to-air victories were claimed by German pilots on 25 August, leaving Hitler

Above: *Junkers Ju 87B Stuka dive-bombers prepare to attack a Republican stronghold in Spain, 1938. The Stuka proved to be a particularly effective weapon in Spain, demoralising enemy soldiers as it screamed down to attack them.*

Left: *Bombs are laid out beneath the wing of a Junkers Ju 87B Stuka. They will be attached to the shackles that can just be discerned in-board of the underwing insignia. Note the stylised pig (nicknamed 'Jolanthe') painted on the wheel cover.*

be known as *Gruppe Eberhardt* (comprising 14 He 51s) and *Gruppe Moreau* (20 Ju 52s and two Heinkel He 70Fs, the latter for reconnaissance). They tended to be deployed as a 'fire brigade', rushing from one part of the front to another as the need arose, and by October they were seeing hard service. Hitler reacted by placing the force on a more regular footing, to be known eventually as the *Legion Kondor* (Condor Legion). In late 1936, this comprised a bomber group (*kampfgruppe*) and a fighter group (*jagdgruppe*), backed by reconnaissance and close support aircraft as well as a flak formation. Commanded by General Hugo Sperrle, the Legion at this stage comprised 120 aircraft and about 5000 men. It was a significant commitment.

But the Legion did not enjoy immediate success. Early bombing raids failed to smash Republican defences around Madrid and, on one occasion, hit Nationalist units waiting to attack. At the same time, the Republicans began to enjoy a measure of air superiority, gained for them by Soviet-supplied (and piloted) fighters such as the Polikarpov I-15 Chato and I-16 Mosca, escorting Tupolev ANT-40 SB *Katyushka* bombers. The He 51s soon showed themselves to be vulnerable, and without guaranteed fighter escort, the Ju 52s switched from daylight to night bombing, with inevitable effects on accuracy and impact. By February 1937, the Legion was looking distinctly battered.

New aircraft in Spain

An overriding need was for more modern aircraft. By early 1937, early versions of the Bf 109 and Ju 87 were being field tested in Spain, but it would be some time before production models would be available in any significant numbers. Meanwhile, however, better bomber designs were coming out of the factories in Germany, enabling the Legion to be re-equipped with Do 17Es, He 111Bs and the first of the Junkers Ju 86Ds. They carried out their first attack in Spain on 9 March; within weeks 16 hastily assembled Bf 109Bs had also arrived, together with Do 17Ps for long-range reconnaissance. It was enough to stave off disaster.

This new commitment was reflected in improvements to Nationalist military efforts, not least in the Basque region in the north. The offensive began on 21 March 1937, when advances were made towards Bilbao, but the main blow fell 10 days later around Republican positions at Orchandiano, in the process of which Legion bombers hit Durango, killing an estimated 250 civilians and injuring probably twice that number. It was a portent of things to come, for as Republican troops gradually fell back towards a 'Ring of Iron' protecting Bilbao, their lines converged on the village of Guernica, where road and rail links crossed the River Oca. On 25 April, Legion reconnaissance aircraft reported heavy military traffic in and around Guernica and the German commander, General Wolfram von Richthofen (cousin of the World War I air ace known as the 'Red Baron') was given permission to carry out a bombing raid. Late in the afternoon 26 bombers (mostly Ju 52s), escorted by 16 fighters, dropped 46 tonnes (45 tons) of bombs on the village, causing widespread damage and up to 1000 (predominantly civilian) deaths.

The effect of Guernica

Once news of the raid broke, there was an international outcry against 'barbaric' methods of war. A haunting mural by the Spanish artist Pablo Picasso ensured that the memory of Guernica remained alive, and the raid was widely regarded as typical of what airpower could and would do. Despite von Richthofen's claim that

Below: A Heinkel He 112B single-seat fighter, one of a number shipped to Spain for evaluation purposes in 1938. Despite their creditable performance, the He 112 was not adopted by the Luftwaffe, which preferred the Messerschmitt Bf 109.

the attack was against a legitimate target – enemy force concentrations – the reputation of the Luftwaffe as a devastatingly effective force was undoubtedly enhanced. Other European powers noted the impact of Guernica and their fear of German power increased. Hitler was to exploit this fear in 1938 when he sent troops to enforce an *Anschluss* (political union) with Austria and to occupy parts of Czechoslovakia: neither Britain nor France felt strong enough to risk confrontation if the German response was likely to be aerial bombardment of vulnerable cities.

New aerial tactics

Meanwhile in Spain, the Legion continued to aid the Nationalists, evolving more effective aerial tactics as experience grew. As the Basques fell back into the 'Ring of Iron', for example, He 51 pilots perfected ground-attack techniques known as the *cadenas* (chain). Switched from fighter duties now that the Bf 109 was arriving in greater numbers, He 51s were each fitted with four 10kg (22lb) bombs, plus a droppable fuel tank which would ignite when it hit the ground. Operating in groups of up to nine aircraft, the pilots flew low-level in search of ground targets, dropping their ordnance at a signal from the flight leader and then taking turns to strafe the enemy until their ammunition ran out. It was techniques such as these that enabled the Nationalists to seize Bilbao on 19 June 1937.

Above: Wearing Spanish uniforms and insignia (including the rather incongruous pilot's wings with royal crown above), these members of the Condor Legion are involved in training their allies to fly German aircraft. The adoption of Nationalist uniforms was a cover for Germany's involvement in the war.

Above right: Heinkel He 59B-2 torpedo-bomber and reconnaissance seaplanes of See-Aufklarungsstaffel 88, *decked out in Nationalist colours, return from a mission over the seas around southern Spain, 1937. They began their operations in support of Franco's forces in November 1936.*

Below right: Members of the Condor Legion sing as they march through a Spanish town. The man in the foreground is a radio operator, as denoted by the 'wings' on his right-hand pocket.

The Legion shifted immediately to the Madrid front, where a Republican offensive was developing. Air opposition proved to be more robust than in the north (the first Bf 109 was lost to air combat on 12 July), but the new tactics gradually gave the Nationalists the upper hand. They claimed air superiority on 18 July for a loss of eight of their own aircraft. By then, the Legion was in desperate need of rest and recuperation, but Franco insisted on exploit-

Above: Typical of the fairly rudimentary conditions under which the Condor Legion often operated in Spain, this airstrip is exposed both to the elements and to enemy air attack, implying a time of Nationalist air superiority. The aircraft, an early Heinkel He 111, is waiting to be bombed up.

Left: Heinkel He 111B bombers are lined up for inspection, possibly before leaving Germany for service in Spain, 1938. The 'Eagle and Shield' symbol on the fuselage of the aircraft in the foreground denotes the 4th Staffel *of* Kampfgruppe 88. *Each He 111B was capable of carrying over 1363kg (3000lb) of bombs.*

ing the initiative, shifting back to the north to take Santander in late August. This became the norm: successive offensives in widely dispersed locations, making the most of Legion bombers, fighters and ground-attack machines to disrupt and demoralise the enemy. The Germans continued to enjoy notable victories: on 7 February 1938, Legion fighters attacked a formation of 12 *Katyushkas* and destroyed 10 of them for no loss to themselves, but the pressures were beginning to tell. Some Condor crews were flying up to seven missions a day, often in appalling conditions; the only consolation was that Nationalist pilots, trained in many cases by the Luftwaffe, were now beginning to appear in greater numbers to ease some of the strain.

Such developing self-sufficiency by the Nationalists allowed the Legion to be gradually reduced in size, although not before some hard fighting had taken place. By June 1938, as Franco advanced into Aragon, the Legion's fighter force was looking rather battered (only 16 of its 30 Bf 109s were serviceable), the He 51s were becoming dangerously obsolete even in the ground-attack role and

Above: *Ground crew work to prepare a Heinkel He 111B for a raid on Republican positions in 1938. The first He 111s arrived in Spain in early 1937.*

Below: *Photographed from a neighbouring bomber, a Heinkel He 111B of the 2nd Staffel of Kampfgruppe 88 (denoted by the tail marking) flies towards its target, 1937.*

Left: Werner Molders, photographed in 1941, by which time he was an Oberst (Colonel) with the Knight's Cross of the Iron Cross with Oakleaves, Swords and Diamonds. While leading Jagdgruppe 88 in Spain, he perfected the 'finger four' tactical formation. By July 1941, he had been credited with 115 'kills'.

Below left: The rudder bar of Werner Molders' Nationalist-painted Messerschmitt Bf 109B shows a total of 15 victory bars, each one denoting an enemy aircraft shot down in combat.

Right: The crew of a reconnaissance Dornier Do 17F discuss a forthcoming mission with the officer on the right. Although reconnaissance missions rarely met hard opposition, any warlike mission was a strain, as shown on the pilot's face (centre).

the flak guns were all but worn out. Hitler did continue to send replacements, although the onset of the Austrian and Czech crises diverted his attention (and that of the Luftwaffe) elsewhere. Between July and October 1938, the Legion could field only 70 aircraft to support operations along the River Ebro, losing 10 of them to enemy action. The opportunity was taken to field-test more modern designs such as the Bf 109E, He 111J and Henschel Hs 126A, while the Ju 87 Stuka carried out dive-bombing attacks as early as February 1938, but it was obvious that the Legion was declining in importance. The last Legion missions were flown on 6 February 1939 as Franco thrust into Catalonia; on 26 March the Republicans accepted defeat and surrendered Madrid.

The Legion held its last formal parade in Spain on 22 May 1939; four days later 5136 officers and men sailed for Germany,

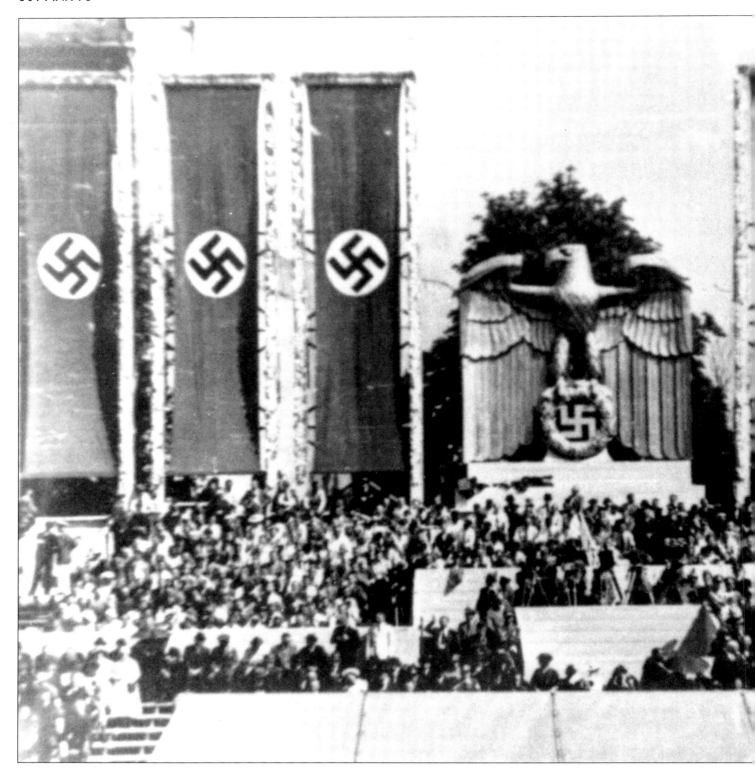

taking with them over 711 tonnes (700 tons) of equipment and most of their remaining aircraft. They could feel proud of their achievements since July 1936. During that time they claimed to have destroyed 386 enemy aircraft (313 of them in aerial combat) for a loss of 232 of their own (of which only 72 were destroyed by enemy action). In addition, over 21,337 tonnes (21,000 tons) of bombs had been dropped by Legion aircraft, contributing in no small way to the eventual Nationalist victory. More sadly, 226 members of the Legion had lost their lives.

Inevitably, valuable lessons were learnt. The most striking was the superiority of German aircraft once second-generation designs had been deployed: the Bf 109 had proved to be superior to nearly all Republican fighters, the Ju 87 had gained a formidable reputation for demoralisation (particularly once sirens and whistles had been added to the aircraft and bombs to increase noise levels), and existing arguments in favour of interdiction bombers had been powerfully reinforced. One result was that Luftwaffe planners placed much more emphasis on bomber production, boosting the

Above: Elements of the Condor Legion, freshly returned from Spain and dressed in new uniforms, march in front of Hermann Göring during a Victory Parade in Hamburg, June 1936.

Left: Crowds of specially invited guests gather for the rather elaborately staged Victory Parade in Berlin to honour returning warriors of the Condor Legion, 6 June 1939.

Below: Members of the Hitler Youth hold up oval placards, each adorned with the name of an airman killed while serving in the Condor Legion, in the Victory Parade in Berlin, 6 June 1939.

whereby pairs of wingmen provided flexible and mutual support in aerial combat. The latter was perfected by Werner Molders when he commanded elements of *Jagdgruppe* 88 in Spain, and this highlights another, equally powerful advantage of the campaign: the existence by 1939 of a cadre of highly skilled and experienced Luftwaffe personnel. They were about to be tested in even more trying campaigns. Spain was no more than a 'rehearsal' for a war that was to see the Luftwaffe rise to a peak of effectiveness and then decline under enemy pressure. It is a dramatic story.

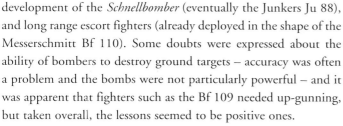

development of the *Schnellbomber* (eventually the Junkers Ju 88), and long range escort fighters (already deployed in the shape of the Messerschmitt Bf 110). Some doubts were expressed about the ability of bombers to destroy ground targets – accuracy was often a problem and the bombs were not particularly powerful – and it was apparent that fighters such as the Bf 109 needed up-gunning, but taken overall, the lessons seemed to be positive ones.

At the same time, tactics had been refined, ranging from the *cadenas* for ground-attack to the 'finger four' fighter technique,

CHAPTER 3

BLITZKRIEG!

The theories of Lightning War that had been developed in Germany, in which the Luftwaffe was a vital element, were put to the test in 1939-40. They achieved stunning successes, and the Luftwaffe was all-conquering.

Left: With engine racing, air-brakes open and siren blaring, a Junkers Ju 87 Stuka releases its centre-line and underwing bombs onto its target during the Polish campaign, September 1939.

Above: A house collapses under aerial bombardment in a suburban district close to Schipol airport, Amsterdam, 10 May 1940. Such destruction was designed to demoralise and disrupt.

Preparations for the German attack on Poland (*Fall Weiss* or 'Plan White') began as early as April 1939, in the immediate aftermath of Hitler's successful seizure of Czechoslovakia. The Luftwaffe's role was a straightforward one of supporting the field armies as they advanced towards Warsaw. General Albert Kesselring's *Luftflotte 1* was to help General Fedor von Bock's Army Group North as it cut the Polish Corridor to Danzig from Pomerania and thrust out of East Prussia towards Warsaw, the

Above: As the early morning mist clears on a Polish airfield in September 1939, a Luftwaffe sentry stands guard over a pair of Junkers Ju 87 Stukas. The white cross just ahead of the cockpit was a recognition symbol used by the Wehrmacht in Poland.

Above left: Luftwaffe ground personnel wait to board transport ships that will carry them into a Polish port, September 1939. Once in Poland, their tasks will include the creation and defence of airfields as well as the maintenance of aircraft.

Below left: The pilot and gunner of a Dornier Do 17P reconnaissance aircraft are photographed in the cockpit during the campaign in Poland. The men are clearly posing for the camera and are probably not even airborne.

Polish capital. General Alexander Lohr's *Luftflotte 4* was to support General Gerd von Rundstedt's Army Group South as it struck northeastwards out of Silesia and Slovakia.

Air reconnaissance missions began in July with the aim of identifying Polish airfields, preparatory to a 'crushing blow' that would destroy the Polish Air Force and gain air superiority for the Luftwaffe. It was widely recognised that the side with freedom of the air would have immediate advantages: it would be able to observe enemy dispositions, call in 'flying artillery', cut the enemy off from his support and use air transport for resupply, while deny-

ing the same to the opposition. As the Polish Air Force had fewer than 1900 aircraft (including reserves) at its disposal in 1939, against which the Germans could field 2152 Luftwaffe and 30 Slovak machines, the majority of which were modern, battle-tested designs, the chances of satisfying such a doctrine seemed high. 'Plan White' began early on 1 September 1939. The air campaign did not get off to a good start, for instead of the Luftwaffe massing its bombers against Polish airfields in a pre-emptive strike, most of the aircraft stayed where they were, grounded by fog and morning mist. By midday, only five or six *gruppen* had carried out their missions, hitting pre-selected airfields around Warsaw, only to find that the bulk of the Polish Air Force had dispersed. Nevertheless, some close air support attacks were mounted, despite the lack of safety guarantees, and German ground units soon began to advance deep into western Poland.

The Luftwaffe establishes air superiority

This became the pattern for the next few days – Luftwaffe bombers struck at airfields but destroyed relatively few enemy aircraft, while Hs 123s supported the army – though by 3 September Göring was confident enough to announce that air superiority had been gained. In response, both Kesselring and Lohr shifted their emphasis to attacks on the Polish Army, cutting its lines of communication and supply. They enjoyed some success. Attacks on the Polish railway system between 2 and 5 September, for example, led to bottlenecks, which were then bombed mercilessly. In other Luftwaffe victories, the Polish 13th Division was virtually destroyed en route to the frontline, while Cavalry Brigade *Kresowa* was badly hit as it detrained. At the same time, airfields continued to be attacked, undermining the overall effectiveness of the Polish Air Force by disrupting its support elements, and Polish aircraft, outnumbered and outclassed, were gradually neutralised. By 5 September, the Luftwaffe was running out of worthwhile targets.

Ground-to-air liaison problems

But the campaign was not free from problems. Although von Richthofen's Stukas proved their worth, helping to destroy Polish defences in the path of the armoured spearheads, ground-to-air co-ordination was poor, leading to some mistakes. On 8 September, for example, just as the tanks of 1st Panzer Division were about to cross the River Vistula, Stukas swooped down to destroy the bridges in front of them. Equally significantly, Luftwaffe support units, trained to cover about 8km (five miles) a day to set up new airfields and communications posts, suddenly found themselves lagging behind an advance that was covering five times that distance. Fuel shortages were one of the results, curtailing the number of sorties that could be flown, and Ju 52s had to be utilised to deliver jerrycans of petrol to forward airstrips.

Even so, the advance into Poland continued at a lightning pace, and once the Soviets had joined in, advancing from the east on 17 September in accordance with the terms of a pact with Hitler signed the previous month, there was little the Poles could do to stave off disaster and ultimate defeat. A Luftwaffe raid on Warsaw on 25 September, carried out in response to Hitler's insistence that the city should fall to German rather than Soviet forces, finally broke the back of any resistance. As remnants of the Polish Air Force flew to neutral Romania, Hungary and Latvia, the Polish Government ceased military operations. By then, the Luftwaffe had lost 285 aircraft destroyed and 279 badly damaged, with 759 personnel killed or missing. In return, its reputation as a ruthless

and effective arm of the German war machine had been considerably enhanced.

Such a reputation was invaluable in the West, where Britain and France had declared war on Germany on 3 September, for it helped to deter any attacks on Germany from that direction while

Above: The Germans do not have it all their own way in Poland, as this shot-down Heinkel He 111P bomber shows. As can be seen, it has undergone some changes to design since the Spanish Civil War, most notably in the heavily glazed nose.

Left: Luftwaffe armourers work to prepare a Messerschmitt Bf 110 long-range fighter for offensive operations, Poland, September 1939. The belts of ammunition are being checked before they are loaded into the nose cavity that houses the main armament of four 7.9mm machine guns. It is a laborious process.

Below right: Henschel Hs 123A single-seat dive-bomber and close-support aircraft, photographed in pre-war livery, 1937. Hs 123As were still in front-line service with the Luftwaffe in 1939, operating as part of Luftflotte 4 *in Poland. They achieved some ground-attack success despite their obvious obsolescence.*

the Polish campaign continued. Politicians in London and Paris, fearful of Luftwaffe raids on cities that it was believed could not be adequately defended, remained cautious, restricting their own air-power to leaflet drops over Germany and attacks on shipping in the North Sea. In the latter process, Allied air forces suffered significant losses. On 18 December 1939, for example, 14 Royal Air Force (RAF) Wellington bombers were lost out of a force of 24, all of them falling to Bf 110 twin-engined fighters. This merely reinforced existing fears about Luftwaffe strength. It was just as well, for the Polish campaign had left Göring's airmen exhausted and dangerously short of munitions.

Plans for 'Plan Yellow'

But Hitler was not one to rest on his laurels. As early as 27 September, he announced his intention to carry out an immediate attack on the West, exploiting the momentum of victory. Codenamed *Fall Gelb* ('Plan Yellow'), this would entail an advance into the neutral Low Countries before sweeping south to take Paris and catch the French Maginot Line defences along the German border in the rear. Once again, Luftwaffe roles would be to gain air superiority and support the ground attack, although an added refinement would be the use of airborne troops to seize key bridges and fortresses in the immediate path of the armour, preventing the creation of enemy blocks. The date for the assault was

initially 12 November, but a combination of factors, including poor weather, production delays and opposition from the generals, led to postponements. On 27 December, Hitler insisted on the attack taking place sometime between 9 and 14 January 1940, and for once it looked as if this would be the case.

'Cut of the Scythe'

On 10 January, however, a Messerschmitt Bf 108 liaison aircraft, flying from Münster to Cologne, went seriously off-course and crash-landed at Mechelin-sur-Meuse in neutral Belgium. On board was a Major Helmut Reinberger who, against strict instructions, was carrying a key part of the *Fall Gelb* planning document. Despite his desperate attempts to burn the incriminating evidence of Hitler's intention to invade Belgium, enough of the document survived to compromise the campaign plan. Hitler was apoplectic when he heard the news, and although there is no direct evidence to suggest that he immediately scrapped existing plans, the incident did allow General Erich von Manstein, Chief of Staff to Army Group A, to put forward an alternative proposal. Known as *Sichelschnitt* ('Cut of the Scythe'), this envisaged an attack into the Low Countries to fix Allied armies in the north while armoured divisions infiltrated the supposedly 'impassable' Ardennes, crossed the River Meuse and cut through to the Channel coast behind the main enemy forces. Cut off from their reserves and supplies,

Above: A practice torpedo (denoted by its painted nose) is carefully loaded aboard a Heinkel He 115B floatplane during evaluation trials, 1940. The He 115 saw operational service in Norway on both sides (the Norwegians had purchased examples pre-war) – it led to some confusion.

Above left: A Luftwaffe anti-aircraft gunner, his Maschinengewehr (MG) 34 ready beside him, watches for enemy air attack as troops and supplies are off-loaded in a southern Norwegian port, April 1940. The German ability to seize Norway depended on sea transport.

Right: General Albert Kesselring, photographed in 1936 when serving as Chief of Staff to the Luftwaffe. Transferred to operational command in 1937, he later commanded Luftflotte 1 in Poland and Luftflotte 2 in the Low Countries and during the Battle of Britain.

British and French armies in Belgium would be encircled and forced to surrender. It was a bold plan, adopted officially in February 1940.

Before this could be put into effect, however, Hitler was persuaded that attacks on Denmark and Norway were essential, both to prevent Allied occupation of those countries and, in the case of Norway, to ensure German access to vital iron-ore deposits. Codenamed *Weserübung* ('Weser Exercise'), the attacks were expected to be short and decisive, paving the way to the main assault on France and the Low Countries without wasting valuable resources. Luftwaffe units would contribute by destroying the relatively tiny Danish and Norwegian Air Forces, after which airborne troops would be flown in to seize bridges and, most importantly, airfields in support of ground units. As a result, the emphasis was firmly on the provision of transport squadrons, protected by long-range fighters and bombers – a total of over 700 aircraft.

The airborne assault on Scandinavia

The attacks began on 9 April 1940. In Denmark, paratroopers seized Aalborg airfield in northern Jutland, allowing infantry units to be flown in, and a force of 28 He 111s dropped leaflets over Copenhagen. This proved to be sufficient to deter the Danes, who surrendered before the end of the day. Simultaneously, Bf 110s landed at Fornebu, outside Oslo, to secure the airfield for Ju 52s

Above: Men of the Reichsarbeitsdienst (RAD), or State Labour Service, help to repair and extend the captured airfield at Oslo-Fornebu, April 1940. Here, they are carrying wooden segments of planking that will be employed to extend the runway, enabling it to be used by twin-engined Bf 110s.

Right: While the runway at Oslo-Fornebu is being laboriously extended, officers supervise the construction of large wooden hangers. The Luftwaffe was aware that once the winter set in, aircraft such as the Bf 110 would have to be protected from the elements, particularly if maintenance work was needed.

Below: Extending the runway at Oslo-Fornebu meant clearing large rocks from the projected area of extension. Here, RAD men struggle to level the ground, using a pulley to lift heavy obstacles.

Above right: RAD men carry bombs to a waiting Heinkel He 111 – a shot designed to make RAD work seem exciting.

Right: Luftwaffe airfield guards, armed with 7.92mm 98K rifles, pause to watch the servicing of a Messerschmitt Bf 109E fighter, presumably at the now extended airbase at Oslo-Fornebu.

Above: A photograph, taken in the air, looking forward past the pilot in the cockpit of a Heinkel He 111P bomber over France, May 1940. The look of concentration on the face of the navigator/observer suggests that this is an 'action shot'.

Right: The results of a bombing raid on Anglo-French troops using one of the typically straight roads of northern France, May 1940. Having lost air superiority during the first few hours of the German attack, the Allies are powerless to prevent such interdiction. The bombing is exceptionally accurate.

carrying infantry soldiers, and paratroopers seized Sola, close to Stavanger. Amphibious landings at Trondheim, Bergen and Kristiansand completed the coup, while the Luftwaffe sought out and destroyed the Norwegian Air Force, reducing it from 102 to 54 serviceable aircraft in a single day. As transports created an air bridge to bring in reinforcements and further landings were made in the far north at Narvik, Norway seemed doomed.

But the campaign went on for longer than expected, partly because the Norwegians refused to give in and partly because the British and French hurriedly committed troops, which landed at Harstad, Namsos and Andalsnes between 14 and 19 April. These bridgeheads were contained – the British withdrew from Namsos

Above: *German airborne troops jumping over Rotterdam on 10 May 1940. The aircraft they are jumping from is a Junkers Ju 52; in the sky above is a Dutch Fokker G-1 twin-boom fighter.*

Below: *Junkers Ju 87 Stukas taxi forward for refuelling at a captured air base in France, May 1940. The fuel has been delivered in barrels and has to be pumped into the aircraft.*

Above: *One of the major tasks facing the Luftwaffe in any campaign was to disrupt enemy lines of communication. Here, two Luftwaffe officers look over their handiwork after the fighting in France is over, June 1940. The bombers have left these rail lines twisted and unusable, rendering Allied reinforcement plans inoperable.*

Left: *Junkers Ju 87 Stukas return from a raid against enemy positions in France, May 1940. The fact that they can fly in such close formation implies a lack of Allied air opposition, though it is worth noting how archaic the Stuka is in design terms – the fixed undercarriage slows the aircraft significantly. However, with total German superiority this did not matter.*

and Andalsnes in early May – but the Luftwaffe had to increase its commitment quite significantly, flying well over 1000 sorties in direct support of ground units. Even then, the danger was not over, for Allied attacks on Narvik necessitated the use of Ju 52s to reinforce the isolated German garrison there between 15 April and 2 June. In the event, Narvik did fall to the Allies on 28 May, only to be abandoned in response to looming disaster in France. By then, the Luftwaffe had lost 260 aircraft in Scandinavia, including 86 invaluable transports.

The Luftwaffe in France

Fall Gelb was initiated on 10 May 1940 and went according to plan. At dawn, 500 Luftwaffe bombers (part of a force that numbered 3868 aircraft against a combined Allied strength of 2600) hit 47 airfields in northern France, 15 in Belgium and 10 in the Netherlands, inflicting significant damage. By the end of the day, Göring's airmen had destroyed 83 Belgian, 62 Dutch and 65 French aircraft, gaining a degree of air superiority that was quickly exploited. At the same time, airborne troops seized bridges over the River Waal and airfields close to The Hague, disrupting Dutch mobilisation, and in an audacious move gliders landed engineers on top of the key Belgian fortress of Eben Emael, covering the approaches to Maastricht. Eben Emael fell on 11 May, opening the way for armoured units to thrust deep into Belgium, and this persuaded the Allies that the original *Fall Gelb* plan was being executed. As anticipated by von Manstein, they moved the bulk of their mobile forces north to meet the threat. Meanwhile, General Ewald von Kleist's panzer group of seven divisions was moving slowly through the 'impassable' Ardennes. Infantry troops were airlifted ahead in Fieseler Fi 156 *Storch* light aircraft to seize road junctions and bridges, allowing the spearheads to approach the barrier of the River Meuse late on 12 May. Once across, they could lance westwards to carry out the *Sichelschnitt* move. However, the execution of opposed crossings, at Montherme, Dinant and Sedan, was not going to be easy. Luftwaffe support was essential. At Sedan, where General Heinz Guderian's XIX Panzer Corps was preparing to cross on 13 May, a four-hour blitz by Stukas and level-bombers paved the way for engineers and infantry to establish bridgeheads and build pontoons for the tanks and artillery. It

Below: Bomb damage in the French town of Sedan, photographed in June 1940. Sedan was the scene of Guderian's assault crossing of the River Meuse in May – a key element in the execution of the Sichelschnitt *plan – and the Luftwaffe had devoted considerable support to his attack. The results of the Luftwaffe attack are apparent.*

Left: Walter Oesau, photographed in August 1940 after the award of the Knight's Cross to the Iron Cross (shown around his neck). By then, Oesau had shot down 20 enemy aircraft in combat, some of them during the Spanish Civil War.

Right: A Fieseler Fi 156 Storch (Stork) short take-off and landing light aircraft flies over an advancing panzer division, May 1940. The advantage of such an aircraft is apparent: the pilot can observe progress and report any forthcoming obstacles to ground commanders. The Storch was favoured by Erwin Rommel.

Below: A Heinkel He 100D single-seat fighter, seen in full Luftwaffe colours over the Channel in 1940. This is pure propaganda, designed to persuade the British that a new aircraft is being deployed (which succeeded in its aim of deceiving the enemy about the number of operational Luftwaffe units). In fact, the He 100 never fired its guns in anger, being something of a failure in design terms.

was an all-arms effort, but one in which the air attacks, demoralising French defenders to the extent of causing them to panic and run, were crucial. On 13 May alone, *Fleigerkorps II* flew a total of 1770 sorties in support of Guderian, following this up with further attacks as the Allies finally realised the danger and reacted by sending their air forces to destroy the Meuse bridges. A combination of anti-aircraft fire and fighter protection led to the destruction of 48 British and six French light bombers on 14 May.

Events farther north continued to fix Allied armies in place. On 14 May Rotterdam was bombed, causing 800 civilian deaths and leading directly to a Dutch decision to surrender, while German ground units continued to advance into Belgium. This allowed von Kleist's panzers to cut across the rear of the Allied armies without encountering strong opposition. Guderian reached the coast at Abbeville on 20 May, then turned north to squeeze the Allies from the rear. Under pressure from north and south, the Allies began their retreat to the beaches at Dunkirk. Göring, anxious to emphasise the power of the Luftwaffe, persuaded Hitler to halt the panzers and allow the bombers to destroy the trapped armies. Between 24 May and 2 June, wave after wave of bombers flew over

Dunkirk, only to encounter RAF Spitfires from southern England (Göring managed to concentrate some 500 fighters and 300 bombers against the Allies at Dunkirk, though many units had mechanical problems). Furious air battles led to the loss of over 100 Luftwaffe machines and diverted the bombers sufficiently to allow over 336,000 Allied soldiers to be evacuated from the beaches. By then, Belgium had surrendered.

Thus by early June the Germans had won a stunning victory, destroying the main Allied formations and opening the way to a thrust south towards Paris. Again, the Luftwaffe contributed, hit-ting Allied units as they pulled back and disrupting rear areas by mounting attacks on communication and supply lines. On 14 June, Paris fell and eight days later the French asked for an armistice. The fighting ended officially on 24 June, by which time the Luftwaffe had lost 1428 aircraft – about 28 per cent of the total deployed since 10 May – and 1722 personnel killed. It was a rela-tively small price to pay for a campaign that had seized Belgium, Luxembourg and the Netherlands, forced the surrender of France and left Britain apparently defenceless. The next logical step – an invasion of Britain – seemed only a matter of time.

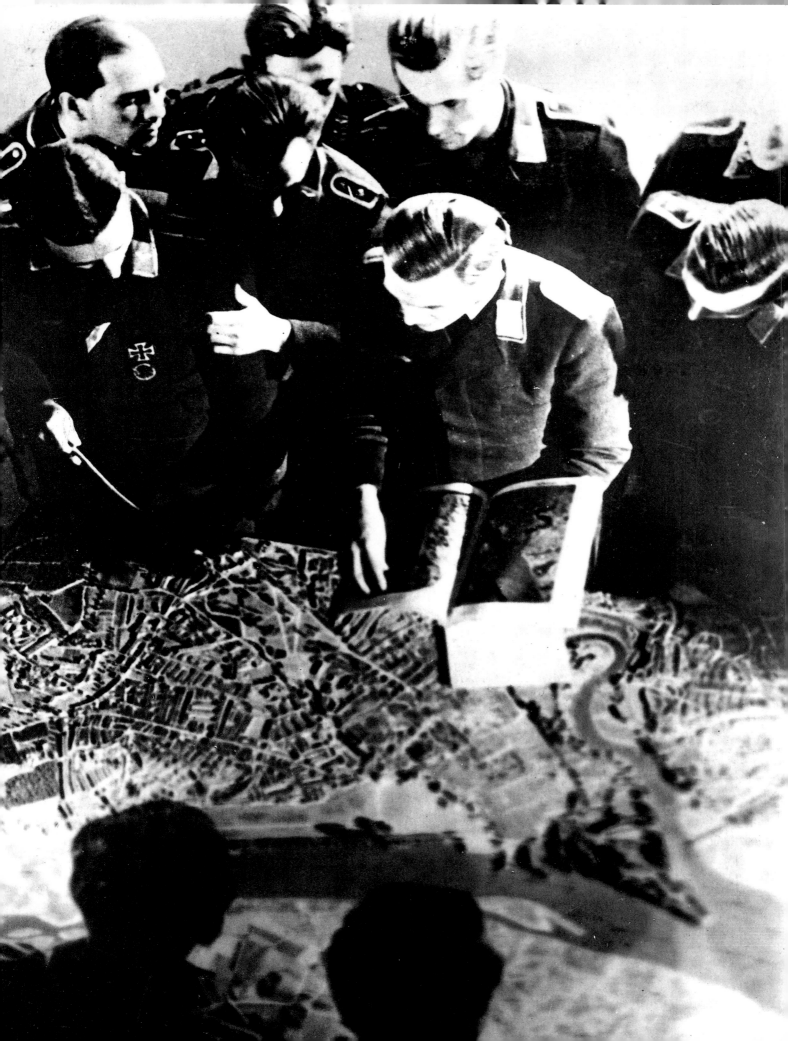

FIRST SETBACK – THE BATTLE OF BRITAIN

Göring was confident that his airmen could smash the Royal Air Force as a prelude to the German invasion of Britain. But a combination of poor command decisions and the tenacity of Britain's pilots stopped the Luftwaffe.

Left: Luftwaffe crews study a model of the port of Southampton, 24 September 1940. The specific target is an aircraft factory.

Above: An He 115 floatplane attacks a British merchant ship in the Channel, July 1940. Channel attacks failed to entice the RAF.

Pre-war studies by the Luftwaffe had concluded that aerial attacks on Britain would be of little strategic value unless air-bases were available in northern France and the Low Countries. Otherwise, most of the worthwhile targets across the Channel would be out of range of existing aircraft (particularly fighters), and the most that might be achieved was for the Luftwaffe to contribute, with the Kriegsmarine (German Navy), to an economic blockade of Great Britain. Indeed, this was what Hitler ordered Göring to do as early as September 1939, when war broke out. Throughout the 'Phoney War' period both Kriegs-marine and Luftwaffe aircraft carried out mining sorties close to British ports, attacked coastal convoys when they came within range, and sought out elements of the British fleet, either in harbour or on the high seas.

The effects were not significant, though in the process of the campaign the Luftwaffe did gradually assume duties that had previously been the preserve of the Kriegsmarine, whose floatplanes and flying boats soon proved inadequate. In the spring of 1940, for example, the Luftwaffe began to deploy Focke-Wulf Fw 200 Condor long-range converted airliners for maritime reconnaissance and attack. Capable of carrying a 909kg (2000lb) bomb load over a radius of 1609km (1000 miles), the four-engined Condors were to prove the 'Scourge of the Atlantic', hitting merchant ships or guiding U-boats in their direction, but there were never enough of them to be decisive. It was another case of too little, too late.

The first raids against England

The strategic situation changed in June 1940, for once the panzers had spearheaded the seizure of both France and the Low Countries, the Luftwaffe was presented with airbases within 20 minutes' flying time of southern England. At the same time, aircraft in Norway and Denmark could reach eastern England, increasing the diversity of the threat. As early as 5 June, about 50 He 111s were sent to hit airfields and military installations in southern England, and these 'nuisance raids' were to continue, mostly at night, for the best part of a week. In the process, the bombers tested their top secret *Knickebein* (Crooked Leg) radio-directional navigation aid, the discovery and countering of which was to constitute an early, albeit unsung, victory for British scientists.

But this was not what Göring had planned. On 30 June, he issued a 'General Directive for the Operation of the Luftwaffe

Above: A fine study of a Heinkel He 111H bomber of **Kampfgeschwader** *26 as it approaches the English coast, August 1940. The band around the fuselage is for recognition purposes, while the letters 'EN' denote the individual aircraft and the* **staffel** *to which it belonged. The* **Geschwader** *code – in this case '1H' – appeared in front of the cross.*

Above right: Close-up of a gunner in the extensively glazed nose compartment of a Heinkel He 111H gives a good indication of the observation he enjoyed. He is armed with a 7.9mm **Maschinengewehr** *(MG) 15 on a special flexible mounting, but is very vulnerable to attack by fighters, especially Royal Air Force Spitfires or Hurricanes. The He 111H series was popular with crews, having pleasant handling qualities, even at maximum weights, plus excellent manoeuvrability and stability. Ironically, the He 111 was designed from the outset to fulfil the roles of both bomber and commercial transport. That said, the two roles were by no means incompatible at the time, as the Nazis always placed an emphasis on military potential in aircraft designs, resulting in some airliners being built in the 1930s which had very dubious commercial value.*

Below right: Luftwaffe ground crew paint a victory symbol on the tail of a Heinkel He 111, denoting in this case the sinking of a British submarine. Such victories were rare – it was difficult to catch a submarine on the surface – hence the looks of satisfaction on the faces of the men involved.

Above: German bombs await transportation to the aircraft that will carry them to England, summer 1940. These are large devices, possibly SC 1000kg (2200lb) bombs, and they are already attached to the shackles which will allow them to be loaded into the bays of Heinkel He 111s or Junkers Ju 88s.

Below: Like ground crews the world over, Luftwaffe armourers and fitters take delight in chalking messages on the bombs that are about to be used. These appear to be SC 500kg (1100lb) blast bombs, about to be loaded into the Junkers Ju 88 parked behind, sometime in the summer of 1940.

against England', reinforcing the need to cooperate closely with the navy in imposing an economic blockade, but for the first time including as a priority the destruction of the Royal Air Force (RAF) and its supporting aircraft industry. These instructions were translated into orders by the Luftwaffe General Staff on 11 July, and sent to *Luftflotte 5* in Norway (commanded by General Hans Jurgen Stumpff), *Luftflotte 2* to the north of Le Havre (under General Albert Kesselring) and *Luftflotte 3* to the south of Le Havre (under General Hugo Sperrle). All three air fleets were to mount attacks designed to force the RAF to react, upon which British aircraft would be destroyed, opening the way to a blockade.

Initial phase of the Battle of Britain

This preliminary phase of what was to be known as the Battle of Britain lasted throughout July and into early August. It was not a success. Small groups of bombers, operating both by day and night, penetrated British defences to hit selected targets, while larger formations, protected by fighters, attacked Channel convoys when they appeared. To the German airmen involved, this was the *Kanalkampf* (Channel War), but it did not force the RAF to engage in all-out battle. Air Chief Marshal Sir Hugh Dowding, commanding RAF Fighter Command, refused to commit his precious Spitfires or Hurricanes unless something like a convoy was actually under attack, and even then was wary about falling into deliberate traps. In the six weeks from 1 July, the Luftwaffe flew over 7000 bomber sorties and dropped 1930 tonnes (1900 tons) of bombs, but the results were disappointing. Although roughly 71,123 tonnes (70,000 tons) of merchant shipping were claimed, the Luftwaffe lost 279 aircraft to the RAF's 142.

On 1 August, Hitler intervened to alter the priorities of the Luftwaffe assault. He was already preparing Operation *Seelöwe* ('Sealion'), an amphibious invasion of England, and realised that any such attack would be doomed unless the forces involved enjoyed both naval and air superiority, at least in the invasion area. Führer Directive No 17, entitled 'For the Conduct of Air and Sea Warfare against England', ordered the Luftwaffe 'to overpower the English Air Force with all the forces at its command', with the attacks directed primarily 'against flying units, their ground installations, and their supply organisations'. Within 24 hours, this had been translated into a Luftwaffe plan codenamed *Adlerangriff* ('Eagle Attack'). According to its details, the *luftflotten* in France and the Low Countries were to spend the first five days of the campaign attacking aircraft, airfields, radar stations and ground facilities in a semi-circle to the west and south of London, out to a radius of about 96km (60 miles); in the following three days, this radius would be brought in to about 48km (30 miles); in the final five days it would squeeze in on London itself. Aircraft from Norway and Denmark would join in to split the British defences by attacking eastern England.

Göring and his commanders had no doubt that this would force Dowding to commit everything he had, and were confident that the Luftwaffe would destroy the RAF with ease. There was some logic to their calculations: on 10 August the three *luftflotten* fielded a total of 3196 aircraft (2485 of which were fully serviceable), against which the RAF in southeast England (constituting No 11 Group under Air Vice Marshal Keith Park) could only deploy 570 Spitfires and Hurricanes (467 of which were serviceable), a few obsolete Fulmars and Defiants and, if any use in the air battles to come, the 500 Hampdens, Wellingtons and Whitleys

Above: A formation of Junkers Ju 87 Stukas, photographed in the summer of 1940 over northern France. The commitment of the Stukas to the Battle of Britain showed how obsolete these aircraft were when pitted against modern interceptor fighters. As losses mounted in August, they were withdrawn from the battle.

Below: A Luftwaffe general (centre, with white lapels) watches as ground crew armourers prepare a 500kg (1100lb) bomb for loading aboard the Heinkel He 111 under which he is standing. The bed of bricks on the bomb-trolley is clearly a local extemporisation for the purposes of the display.

Above: *Messerschmitt Bf 109E fighters stand ready on an airfield in northern France, summer 1940. They belong to* Jagdgeschwader 53, *as denoted by the 'Ace of Hearts' symbol painted on the side of the engine cowling.*

Below: *Striking poses similar to those adopted by RAF fighter pilots on their airfields in southern England, these Luftwaffe pilots of* Jagdgeschwader 3 *wait for their next operation, summer 1940. The pilot seated on the steps is* Unteroffizier Scheef.

Above: As Adolf Galland (left) looks on, Walter Oesau is presented to the Führer. Oesau is about to receive the Swords to his Knight's Cross in recognition of having downed 40 enemy aircraft. Galland has just received the same award.

Below: Luftwaffe armourers carefully load a belt of 7.9mm bullets into a machine gun mounted alongside the nose of a German fighter. Care is essential if the pilot is not to be plagued by stoppages in mid-combat – a potentially fatal occurrence.

Above: Adolf Galland, one of the leading fighter 'aces' of the Battle of Britain.
Photographed as an Oberst (Colonel), he is wearing the Knight's Cross with Oakleaves and Swords at his neck.

Below: Unteroffizier (Corporal) Buchholz works on Sochatzy's 'Tizi', summer of 1940, making sure that it is fully prepared for action at the shortest notice. He is responsible for checking all aspects of the aircraft, including the engine, airframe and guns.

Above: Staffelkapitan (Staff Captain) Kurt Sochatzy (right) of Jagdgeschwader 3 poses with his mechanic, Unteroffizier Buchholz, in front of his Messerschmitt Bf 109F, nicknamed 'Tizi', in August 1940. The odd-looking bandolier around Sochatzy's lower leg contains ammunition for his flare pistol, vital if he is shot down over the Channel. Many Luftwaffe pilots also wore life jackets when operating over water.

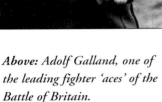

Above: *Major Walter Oesau (centre) shows the strains of command while listening to a conversation between General Osterkamp (left) and the fighter 'ace' Werner Molders (right). Oesau is wearing his recently awarded Knight's Cross.*

Below: *A gathering of eagles: three Knight's Cross winners are photographed together in the summer of 1940. On the left is* Oberstleutnant *(Lieutenant-Colonel) Leie, with Major Oesau in the centre and* Leutnant *Mayer on the right.*

of Bomber Command. On paper, the RAF was outnumbered by at least two to one in fighters and, in overall terms, by a factor of nearly six to one. In addition, Britain's anti-aircraft defences were weak, with only 1200 heavy and 650 light guns protecting London and the Channel ports. It should have been a walkover.

But the British did enjoy certain crucial advantages. Although No 11 Group may have looked weak, it was operating largely over its own soil, meaning that any pilots who did survive being shot down would be available to fly again, and Park could call on reinforcements from other Fighter Groups (No 10 in the west of England and No 12 to the north of London), the bases for which were out of Luftwaffe fighter range or not included in Göring's target list. More importantly, the British had their 'Chain Home' radar system deployed along the southern and eastern coasts, enabling them to foresee the build-up of Luftwaffe raids and so conserve and direct their fighters for maximum effect.

These advantages were shown as the Battle of Britain progressed, though the RAF did come periously close to defeat in the process. Göring initially chose 10 August as the opening date for *Adlerangriff*, but poor weather intervened to delay this for three days. The Luftwaffe did not cease operations during that time; indeed, on 12 August bombers seriously damaged the radar station at Ventnor on the Isle of Wight, opening up a potentially vulnerable gap in the

Above: The scourge of the Luftwaffe in the Battle of Britain: Supermarine Spitfire Mark IAs of No 65 Squadron, RAF Fighter Command, fly in formation over southern England, 1940. With a maximum speed of 580kmph (362mph) and armed with eight .303in machine guns, these were formidable machines. The RAF had 700 fast monoplane fighters by June 1940 – a mixture of Spitfires and Hurricanes, and the factory rates of production were high. By late 1940, for example, British aircraft manufacturing plants were turning out just over 400 fighters a month. In comparison, German industry was producing an average of less than 200 a month.

Above right: Under the watchful eyes of a Military Policeman and a Grenadier Guardsman, the crew of a Luftwaffe aircraft downed over southern England in 1940 enter captivity. The pilot is on the left (as denoted by his breast badge); the Oberfeldwebel on the right has the Iron Cross First Class.

Below right: A Heinkel He 111H lies with its back broken on a Scottish hillside, October 1939. This is a photograph of the first German aircraft to be downed over the British Isles in World War II – hence the considerable interest being displayed. It was credited to Spitfires of Nos 602 and 603 Squadrons.

Above: *The crew of a Heinkel He 111 drink from their thermos flasks having just returned from another raid on southern England, September 1940. Although the flying distances involved were not large, each raid took its toll in terms of stress and fatigue. Adrenalin rushes caused by combat often left crews with raging thirsts – for those who survived, that is.*

Left: *A flight of Messerschmitt Bf 110s photographed over southern England, August 1940. The Bf 110, designed as a long-range fighter, proved to be vulnerable to British single-engined interceptors during the Battle of Britain. In the end, Bf 109s were forced to act as protectors. Fighters defending fighters was not envisaged in pre-war tactics.*

Right: *On 7 September 1940, Göring switched the main weight of his offensive away from RAF airfields and installations to the port of London. This photograph, one of the most famous of World War II, shows the East End aflame. Despite the destruction and loss of civilian life, it gave the RAF the respite it needed. In addition, it had exactly the opposite effect to that intended by the Nazi leadership: instead of blitzing the population into submission, it merely fortified resolve.*

defences – but *Adlertag* ('Eagle Day') was eventually set for 13 August. On that day, the Luftwaffe flew a total of 1485 sorties, only to find that British pilots were able to exploit the early warning system and impose significant casualties, shooting down 20 bombers and 24 fighters in furious air battles for the loss of 13 fighters. More importantly, Göring had already ordered his airmen to concentrate on airfields, and although a number were hit and put out of action, this did mean that radar stations were spared, leaving the system largely intact. The raids continued until 18 August, constituting the second phase of the battle, during which the Luftwaffe lost 247 aircraft to the RAF's 131. What Göring did not realise was that Dowding was beginning to run out of trained pilots (particularly ones who could also lead the squadrons in battle) and was already 'raiding' other Fighter Groups.

The RAF at breaking point

This was shown during the next phase, which lasted from 19 August to 6 September. As the Luftwaffe increased the pressure, flying up to 1000 sorties a day, Göring shifted tactics, deploying more fighters in an attempt to lure the RAF into battle. It almost worked. By 6 September, Dowding had lost a further precious 273 fighters in combat, and though the balance still seemed to be in his favour, with 303 Luftwaffe aircraft downed (including 146 Bf 109s), he was fast running out of reserves. As plans were made to pull the RAF back to the north of London, the Luftwaffe, still fielding 1158 bombers and over 1000 fighters, seemed on the brink of victory.

It was at this point that Göring made a fatal error. Convinced (with good reason) that the Luftwaffe was succeeding, and aiming to demoralise the British people as the next logical preliminary to invasion, he ordered his bombers to concentrate on London. This tied the Luftwaffe to a precise and predictable target and, even more importantly, relieved the pressure on the RAF. As Dowding hastily conserved his remaining assets, absorbing new aircraft and pilots while overseeing the repair of damaged airfields, Göring's airmen turned their attention to a campaign for which they were not really prepared. On 7 September, in a raid lasting nearly 11 hours, some 650 bomber and 1000 fighter sorties were flown over London, the dockland area of which was hit by 670 tonnes (660 tons) of high explosive and thousands of incendiaries. Nearly 450 Londoners were killed, but the Luftwaffe lost 36 aircraft and gave notice of their future intentions.

The raids allowed Dowding to concentrate his forces to protect the capital. The advantages became apparent on 15 September (later adopted as official 'Battle of Britain Day'), when successive Luftwaffe raids were met by swarms of fighters, some brought in from No 12 Group. For the loss of 26 aircraft, the RAF managed to destroy 58 of the enemy. This pattern soon became the norm. Between 16-30 September, Dowding lost 115 aircraft to the Luftwaffe's 199, and it was obvious that the initiative had been wrested from the Germans. Hitler, already thinking about his projected assault on the Soviet Union, cancelled 'Sealion', while Göring, aware that his forces would soon be called upon to support that venture, downgraded the daylight attacks on Britain to

fighter-bomber sweeps using Bf 109s and Bf 110s in roles for which they were not designed.

But British victory in the Battle of Britain did not mean that German attacks ceased. Despite the losses over London in mid-September, Göring continued to press for a bombing campaign. Indeed, by the end of the month 6953 British civilians had been killed in Luftwaffe raids and British anti-aircraft defences had proved to be weak. These considerations led to a shift in tactics, with the bombers being sent over by night to hit targets through-out the country. It seemed to work. As searchlights swept the night skies fruitlessly, anti-aircraft guns failed to do much damage and British night-fighters, lacking radar, had little impact. This was shown most dramatically on the night of 14/15 November 1940, when 439 German bombers, spearheaded by 'pathfinder' aircraft equipped with a sophisticated radio-direction beam known as *X-Gerät*, dropped 511 tonnes (503 tons) of high explosive and over 30,000 incendiaries on the city of Coventry in the industrial Midlands. The raid killed 568 people and left 1256 badly injured; more than 60,000 buildings were destroyed or damaged and fac-tory production faltered.

Nor was Coventry the only target. By Christmas 1940, Birmingham, Sheffield, Liverpool and Manchester had been badly hit, and other cities were beginning to feel the weight of Luftwaffe attacks. At the same time, raids on London continued. On the night of 29/30 December, 130 bombers hit the city, dropping incendiaries that left an area between St Paul's Cathedral and the Guildhall aflame. Britain was effectively under siege.

Above: British troops stand guard over the remains of a Dornier Do 17Z shot down at Leaves Green, close to Biggin Hill airbase, on 18 August 1940. Despite the extensive damage to the cockpit area, the five-man crew survived.

But Britain did survive. Its population, more enraged than demoralised by the raids, insisted on conducting 'business as usual' and, as the attacks were absorbed, countermeasures were adopted. British scientists learnt to 'jam' the German radio-direction beams, and even on occasion to 'bend' them to ensure that the bombers dropped their loads on open ground; at the same time, anti-air-craft guns and searchlights became more effective and night-fight-ers, equipped with on-board radar, began to seek out and destroy their prey. The Blitz continued until the very eve of the attack on the Soviet Union – as late as 10/11 May 1941 more than 1400 civilians were killed in London – but by then it was obvious that the Luftwaffe had failed. It had not destroyed the RAF, nor had it prepared the way for an invasion. It was Göring's first setback and one that gave the lie to pre-war theories that countries could be defeated from the air. However awe-inspiring the Luftwaffe may have been over Guernica, Warsaw or Rotterdam, none of these cities had been adequately defended, chiefly because air superiori-ty had been lost before the raids began. Over Britain, Göring's error was to shift to city bombing before his enemy's air force had been neutralised. It was a fatal error, leaving Britain undefeated in the West at a time when Hitler was insistent on shifting his attacks to the East, against the Soviet Union.

Left: *Caught on camera by the attacking fighter, this Messerschmitt Bf 110 is about to be shot down. A lack of manoeuvrability and speed meant that the Bf 110 was not able to survive against more agile fighters, while its rearward-facing defensive armament was inadequate.*

Below: *The Messerschmitt Bf 109E of* Oberleutnant *Karl Fischer of* Jagdgeschwader 27 *is recovered from Windsor Great Park, early October 1940. Fischer survived his fight with the RAF.*

CHAPTER 5

THE DESERT WAR

In North Africa the Luftwaffe was hard pressed to keep its aircraft flying in the face of mechanical problems and fuel shortages, and in the end was overwhelmed by Allied aerial superiority.

Left: The crew of a Messerschmitt Bf 110 long-range fighter shelter from the sun, North Africa 1941. By this stage in the war, the Bf 110 was being used more as a fighter-bomber.

Above: A Junkers Ju 88A bomber of Kampfgeschwader 30, *identified by its distinctive* Adler *(Eagle) nose insignia, photographed on an airfield in the Balkans in 1941.*

The Mediterranean area, covering the Balkans, the North African coast and islands in between, had never figured large in Hitler's grand strategy. His alliance with fellow-fascist Benito Mussolini meant that any Allied opposition in the south should have been blocked by the Italians, leaving the Germans to deal with the much more important task of destroying the Soviet Union. Vague ideas of a link-up between German forces advancing through the Caucasus and Middle East and Italians in Egypt and Libya may have been mooted, but they were never taken very seriously. As far as Hitler was concerned, if Mussolini could secure

the southern flank, he would have more than amply satisfied the terms of the Rome-Berlin Axis.

Unfortunately, Mussolini proved incapable of doing this. Although he dutifully declared war on Britain and France in June 1940 (delaying the process until it was obvious that the Allies were on the brink of defeat), his offensives in the Balkans and North Africa were incompetent affairs. In September, he sent his Tenth Army into western Egypt, aiming for the Suez Canal; a month later he rather foolishly invaded Greece. Both offensives quickly ground to a halt and, as both the British and Greeks mounted

The first Luftwaffe raid on Malta took place as early as 9 January 1941, when airfields and harbour facilities were hit, but the campaign was disrupted by Operation 'Barbarossa' (the codename for the invasion of the Soviet Union) in June. Some squadrons were diverted north to take part in 'Barbarossa', while others moved east to bases in Greece, Crete and Rhodes. The intention was to prevent British use of the eastern Mediterranean, through which they might try to carry supplies to their new Soviet allies, utilising the Suez Canal, Dardanelles and Black Sea. Malta was left to the Italians and Rommel was required to make do with less than 150 Stukas and Bf 109s. By then, he had managed to push the British back to the Egyptian-Libyan border, but in the process his supplies, coming along the coast road from Tripoli, were overstretched. In November, after furious tank battles around Tobruk, the British reversed their fortunes and forced Rommel to fall back towards western Cyrenaica. Once there, his supply line became shorter, but with British aircraft now in bases from where they could support their colleagues from Malta, the Mediterranean supply link to southern Italy became vulnerable.

Above: Messerschmitt Bf 110 fighters of Zerstörergeschwader 26 *are lined up, ready for action, in North Africa, 1941. The fact that the aircraft are parked so close together, surrounded by fuel drums, suggests that no-one is expecting enemy air attack.*

counteroffensives, the Italians looked as if they would be destroyed. As early as February 1941, only days after the remnants of the Tenth Army had surrendered to the British at Beda Fomm in Cyrenaica (eastern Libya), Hitler felt obliged to commit German troops (the *Deutsches Afrika Korps* or DAK) under General Erwin Rommel to prevent a complete Italian collapse. Two months later, German troops invaded Yugoslavia and Greece to ensure that the Balkans were clear before the invasion of the Soviet Union began.

Luftwaffe deployment in the Mediterranean

By early 1941, therefore, Luftwaffe squadrons were beginning to be deployed to the Mediterranean. In March, as the Axis alliance was expanded, nearly 500 aircraft (40 bombers, 120 Ju 87s, 120 Bf 109s, 40 Bf 110s and 170 reconnaissance and transport machines) moved to airfields in Romania and Bulgaria, while a further 390 (mostly Ju 87s and Bf 109s) formed *Fliegerkorps X* in southern Italy, Sicily, Sardinia, Greece and North Africa. It was the latter aircraft that were to support Rommel's campaigns in Libya and Egypt, although their tasks were never simply those of close support for ground forces. In addition, and of crucial importance, *Fliegerkorps X* was to help the Italians neutralise the island of Malta, from where British naval and air units were already interdicting supply lines for Axis forces in the North African theatre.

Above: *A Messerschmitt Bf 109G fighter, characterised by its smooth cowling lines and enlarged under-nose air filter, stands on an airfield in Sicily, late 1942. The camouflage scheme breaks up the contours of the aircraft when viewed from the top or side.*

Below: *Although dangerously obsolete in the face of fast interceptor fighters, the Stuka continued to be widely employed. In North Africa, it was still a powerful instrument of demoralisation and destruction, but only if protected.*

Above: *An artist records the scene at Ain el Gazala airfield, mid-1941. The Bf 109E in the foreground belongs to Jagdgeschwader 27, the first deployed to North Africa in April 1941.*

Above right: *A kette (flight) of Ju 87 Stukas returns to its desert base, 1941. The rudimentary nature of the base can be seen, together with its isolation, creating problems of resupply.*

By November 1941, up to two-thirds of the supplies despatched to Rommel from southern Europe were failing to get through, the ships being destroyed by submarine and surface-warship attack, as well as air assault. On 2 December Hitler agreed to act, reinforcing Luftwaffe units in the area and appointing Albert Kesselring (now a field marshal) as Commander-in-Chief South to coordinate Axis efforts. When he arrived in theatre in early January 1942, he had about 650 Luftwaffe aircraft under his immediate command, 260 of them devoted to supporting the DAK in North Africa, where Rommel had wasted no time in mounting a counteroffensive that would soon push the British back to Gazala. In addition, the *Regia Aeronautica* (Italian Air Force) had about 500 assorted bombers and fighters available, though it was recognised that these were generally obsolete designs, incapable of decisive action. If Malta was to be neutralised, it was down to the Luftwaffe to achieve it.

The assault on Malta

The offensive began in mid-January 1942. Initially, raids on the island were spasmodic – by the end of February only about 1016 tonnes (1000 tons) of bombs had been dropped, enabling the British garrison and civilian population to adjust – but in March *Fliegerkorps III* deployed to Sicily, contributing a further 425 aircraft (including 190 bombers and 115 Bf 109s) to the campaign. This meant that the weight of attack could be dramatically increased, starting in March when 2235 tonnes (2200 tons) of bombs were dropped in a total of more than 2800 sorties. British

Right: Han-Joachim Marseille, a Luftwaffe fighter 'ace' known as the 'Star of Africa', views one of his kills – a Hurricane of No 213 Squadron. Marseille was killed on 30 September 1942.

Above: Luftwaffe ground crew refuel a Messerschmitt Bf 110 on a desert airstrip, February 1942. The laborious process of pumping fuel into the tanks of the aircraft can be gauged.

Below: Mechanics work on the Junkers Jumo 211Da 12-cylinder liquid-cooled engine of a Ju 87B. This particular aircraft has been 'tropicalised' by the addition of sand filters.

Above right: By 1942, German resupply difficulties in North Africa were such that every method was used. Here, a Gotha Go 242A glider disgorges its cargo of fuel and other essentials.

Below right: A Heinkel He 111H is bombed-up. The solar topees of the ground crew and tropicalised engines of the aircraft show that the scene is one from the Mediterranean.

airfields and military installations were hit hard, reducing the capacity for defence, and though 60 Luftwaffe aircraft were destroyed between early January and late March 1942 over Malta, this was not sufficient to stop the raids. Indeed, by April the British authorities were concerned enough to evacuate all air and naval assets from the island, leaving the army garrison (a depleted 234 Brigade) to face the onslaught alone. If Kesselring had succeeded in persuading Hitler to mount a projected Italian-German airborne assault (codenamed 'Operation Hercules') in late April, the island would surely have fallen. As it was, a combination of factors – memories of the heavy airborne losses on Crete the previous May, a shortage of transport aircraft due to demands from the Eastern Front, Rommel's sudden advance through the Gazala Line to take Tobruk and move into western Egypt – deterred Hitler from authorising the attack.

But there were other ways in which Kesselring could ensure that pressure was maintained. One of these was to use his considerable air assets against supply convoys moving to the relief of Malta. In March 1942, for example, the British devoted four cruisers, 18 destroyers and an anti-aircraft ship to escort just four merchant ships to the beleaguered island, having to contend with virtually continuous air attack. In August, the situation was even more drastic, with 14 merchantmen being escorted by a veritable fleet of three aircraft carriers, two battleships, six cruisers, 24 destroyers and an anti-aircraft ship. As these vessels ploughed through the western Mediterranean towards their objective, Luftwaffe attacks were so effective that only five of the merchant ships survived.

Above: Luftwaffe personnel check the harnesses of their parachutes before boarding the Junkers Ju 52 transports in the background, Mediterranean theatre 1942. Despite the 'jump boots' being worn, these are not **Fallschirmjäger** (paratroopers).

Below: An early version of the Messerschmitt Me 321 glider, appropriately known as the **Gigant** (Giant), during trials at Leipheim in the summer of 1941. The **Gigant** was designed to carry tanks or self-propelled guns.

Above right: A logical, if somewhat bizarre, development of the Me 321 glider, the Messerschmitt Me 323 had six engines in order to transform it into a transport aircraft. It proved vulnerable: on 22 April 1943 14 were shot down in a single air engagement.

Below right: A Blohm und Voss Bv 222 Wiking (Viking) long-range maritime patrol and reconnaissance flying boat, 1942. This aircraft type was not impressive, but was used to carry emergency supplies from Athens to Derna in Libya in late 1941.

Nevertheless, they delivered enough supplies to ensure that Malta held out, at a time when German attention was already shifting farther east, where Rommel seemed poised to take Alexandria and the Suez Canal. If that happened, Malta would be irrelevant.

High attrition rates

Throughout his campaigns, Rommel had enjoyed a degree of support from the Luftwaffe, particularly in terms of dive-bombers and ground-attack fighters. Organised under *Fliegerführer Afrika*, these aircraft – which rarely totalled more than 200 machines – could never wrest complete air superiority from the British, chiefly because the theatre of operations precluded that, with airfields often extemporised and remote. But in 1941 and again in 1942, the Luftwaffe had provided support when it was needed, sending Ju 87s to bomb British positions with their usual demoralising effects (not least during the siege of Tobruk between April and December 1941), and deploying Bf 109s and some Bf 110s to keep enemy aircraft at bay or to strafe ground positions. On occa-

sions, the size of the Luftwaffe in-theatre had been increased for specific operations, notably in May 1942 when Rommel assaulted the Gazala Line. For that attack, more than 260 aircraft were made available, though throughout the desert war serviceability rates were relatively low, reducing the number of operational aircraft by as much as 40 per cent at times. Heat, dust and sandstorms played havoc with aircraft designed primarily for operations in Europe, and the supply of fuel could not always be guaranteed, especially at times when the Allies were hitting convoys in the central Mediterranean. Nevertheless, when Rommel pushed to the south around the Gazala defences, his bombers flew nearly 1400 sorties to contribute to the neutralisation of the Free French fortress at Bir Hacheim, allowing the offensive to continue.

But the Luftwaffe could not sustain its desert operations once Rommel pushed into Egypt. As his ground forces advanced to the Alamein Line in July 1942, its air support unavoidably lagged behind, lacking fuel supplies and forward maintenance facilities. In desperation, some fuel and spares were flown to Tobruk by Ju

52 transports and Blohm und Voss Bv 222 six-engined flying boats, but the amounts were small and what there was had still to be carried nearly 640km (400 miles) overland to the Axis frontline. At the same time, the British were taking full advantage of their shortened supply lines to build up their strength in Egypt, part of which was an enhanced Desert Air Force. By early September 1942, when Rommel made his last attempt to continue his advance, only to be held by the newly arrived Eighth Army commander, General Bernard Montgomery, at Alam Halfa, the Luftwaffe had been effectively swept from the skies. Nearly two months later, when Montgomery assumed the offensive in the Second Battle of Alamein, the Luftwaffe was outnumbered three to one by British aircraft. There was little that *Fliegerführer Afrika* could do.

Above: As British forces advanced from Alamein into Libya in late 1942, they came across the sad remains of the desert Luftwaffe. Here at Derna, a heavily cannibalised Bf 109 stands next to the burnt-out remains of a Ju 52 hospital transport.

Right: Two Messerschmitt Bf 110s fly in formation close to one of the Aegean islands, late 1943. The one in the foreground carries the code '3U', denoting **Zerstörergeschwader 26**.

Below: Axis defeat in North Africa: British troops have gathered the remains of a host of Luftwaffe (as well as some **Regia Aeronautica**) aircraft, stacking the wings to create a fence around less recognisable material.

But this did not end the fighting in the Mediterranean. Despite the collapse of Mussolini's government in July 1943, leading to an armistice with the Allies in September, German forces occupied Italy and Luftwaffe units continued to support ground forces where and when they could. In Italy itself, this was never easy – the Allies enjoyed numerical and technological air superiority by mid-1943 – but occasionally successes occurred. One of these was in the fighting for the Dodecanese Islands in late 1943, when ill-judged British attempts to seize the islands from their Italian garrisons were countered. For a time, Luftwaffe aircraft reasserted their strength, hitting outlying islands and British warships with Ju 87s and Ju 88s preparatory to landings on Kos and Leros, carried out in part by Luftwaffe paratroopers withdrawn from Greece. But this was a rare victory, caused principally by American refusals to support the British in what they saw as a peripheral campaign, leaving their allies overstretched and vulnerable. Elsewhere, by 1943 the Mediterranean was essentially an Allied 'lake', with the Luftwaffe assets still in-theatre outclassed. By then, of course, Hitler had other worries, not least on the Eastern Front, where Soviet forces were gradually turning the tables, and over Germany itself, where Anglo-American bombers were beginning to have an effect on the war effort. The Luftwaffe had much more important duties to perform.

Rommel accepted defeat at Alamein on 4 November, beginning a retreat that presaged the end of the desert war. Four days later, Anglo-American forces mounted amphibious landings in French Northwest Africa (Morocco and Algeria) under the codename Operation 'Torch'. As they advanced into Tunisia, Rommel's rear was threatened, forcing him to abandon the whole of Libya to Montgomery's men. Hitler rather belatedly realised that the Mediterranean was about to be lost, opening up the 'soft underbelly' of Europe to Allied assault, and suddenly found reserves of aircraft which, if made available earlier, might have made a significant difference. Altogether, just under 1000 Luftwaffe machines – 850 in Sicily, Sardinia and Tunisia, and 120 in southern France (occupied by the Germans in the immediate aftermath of 'Torch') – were deployed in an effort to halt the Allied advances. To a certain extent they succeeded, helping to stall the Anglo-American forces in the mountains of Tunisia, but the usual problems of fuel supply and maintenance still pertained.

By February 1943 *Fliegerführer Afrika* was down to 150 aircraft (mostly Bf 109s), and the recently formed *Fliegerführer Tunisia* had only 140 (including a small number of the new Focke-Wulf Fw 190 fighters). The two commands were amalgamated once Rommel retreated into southern Tunisia, but it was apparent there was little anyone could do to stave off defeat. By May the Allies were closing relentlessly on Tunis, and attempts were made to withdraw key personnel by air using Ju 52s and even Messerschmitt Me 323 *Gigant* (Giant) powered gliders. The results were disastrous, with such aircraft falling easily to Allied fighters. Surviving aircraft were withdrawn to Sicily and southern Italy as Tunis fell on 7 May. Five days later, the war in North Africa was over.

STORM IN THE EAST

During the first few weeks of Operation 'Barbarossa', the German attack on Russia, the Luftwaffe achieved total air superiority. Thousands of Soviet aircraft were destroyed on the ground in a stunning story of success.

Left: Burning oil-storage tanks mark the aftermath of a Luftwaffe raid during the early stages of 'Barbarossa', July 1941. Destruction of such targets was a vital role of the Luftwaffe.

Above: The Stukas strike! On 22 June 1941, as Operation 'Barbarossa' begins, the Ju 87s carry out their usual tasks: seeking out enemy force concentrations and demoralising enemy troops.

Preparations for Operation 'Barbarossa' began as early as September 1940, while the Luftwaffe was still fighting the Battle of Britain, and precise operational directives were issued two months later. According to Hitler's Directive No 21, dated 18 December 1940, Luftwaffe roles in the invasion of the Soviet Union were to be familiar ones: 'It will be the duty of the Air Force to paralyse and eliminate the effectiveness of the Russian Air Force as far as possible ... it will also support the main operations of the Army.' Just as in Poland, Scandinavia and France, Göring's airmen were to carry out pre-emptive air strikes against

the enemy air force, gaining air superiority that would enable them to use their bombers and fighters to hit lines of communication and supply, isolating the battlefield and opening up enemy ground forces to direct air assault.

In the case of the Soviet Union, however, this was a tall order. Hitler was insistent on a short, sharp campaign – he called for the capture of Leningrad in the north, Moscow in the centre and the Ukraine in the south before the winter weather curtailed operations – for which he recognised the need to increase the size of his ground forces by raising 40 new divisions. The demands that such

an increase made on German industry meant that the Luftwaffe had to take second place to the army. Aircraft losses incurred in the West were to be replaced, but no augmentation was authorised and, of significance for the future, the introduction of new aircraft designs was delayed. This meant that, by June 1941, Luftwaffe frontline strength was little more than it had been in early 1940: 3340 bombers and fighters. Moreover, the duties to be carried out by air units had escalated considerably: 780 aircraft had now to be maintained in the West, plus 370 in the Mediterranean and nearly 200 for the air defence of Germany itself, leaving less than 2000 combat aircraft for 'Barbarossa'. This figure did not include transports, liaison aircraft or reconnaissance machines, nor did it reflect the contributions that Germany's allies could make, but even when every aircraft type was counted, the total in the East still came to only 3900. At a conservative estimate, the Soviets then had 7500 aircraft in their western theatre and a further 2500 in the Far East. Though many were obsolete designs, the numerical balance seemed to be tilted seriously against the Luftwaffe.

The Luftwaffe in the Balkans

Nor were these the only problems facing the Luftwaffe in 1941, for as the preparations for 'Barbarossa' went ahead, Göring suddenly found himself ordered to support an attack in the Balkans. Italy's failures in North Africa and Greece left the southern flank of any German assault into the Soviet Union potentially vulnerable, forcing Hitler to send assistance to his fascist ally. Rommel's arrival in Libya undoubtedly saved the situation in North Africa, but the Balkans were a different matter. Not only were Greek

Opposite above: A Junkers Ju 87B of **Stukageschwader 3** *on an airfield in the Balkans in 1941. It is waiting to be 'bombed-up' before taking part in the final stages of the short campaign to subdue Yugoslavia. The nose and tail fin would be bright yellow.*

Opposite below: General Eduard Dietl (right, with parachute) waits to board a Junkers Ju 52 transport, May 1941. Dietl commanded the **Gebirgsjäger** *(Mountain Troops) of the German Army (as denoted by the* **Edelweiss** *badge on his cap), elements of which took part in the invasion of Crete.*

Right: A dramatic sequence of photographs shows the destruction of HMS Gloucester, *a Royal Navy Southampton-class cruiser, sunk by air attack off Crete on 22 May 1941. The air-sea battle around Crete was a major success for the Luftwaffe: its bombers sank three cruisers and six destroyers in a series of furious engagements. In addition, the Royal Navy had a further five battleships and an aircraft carrier damaged. The British lost 25,000 men in the campaign in the Balkans.*

forces threatening to push Mussolini's troops back into Albania but, in late March 1941, a revolution in Yugoslavia removed the pro-Axis monarch, raising the spectre of Allied intervention. One of the first countermoves ordered by Hitler was the reinforcement of Luftwaffe units already in Bulgaria and Romania, raising the number of combat aircraft there to over 600.

Victory in the Balkans

It was these aircraft, plus others flying out of Austria and Hungary, that spearheaded the assault on Yugoslavia and Greece, initiated on 6 April 1941. They gained air superiority with commensurate ease: *Luftflotte 4*, comprising a total of 1090 German aircraft, with 660 Italian machines in support, faced no more than 400 Yugoslav and 80 Greek aircraft, many of them of obsolete design. Air strikes early on 6 April caught most of the enemy aircraft on the ground and destroyed them, enabling *Luftflotte 4* to concentrate immediately on providing close support to ground units. Duties included reconnaissance, ground attack and long-range interdiction, the latter involving the destruction of troop concentrations, bridges, roads and railways, and the bombing of Belgrade. The campaign was remarkably short and very successful. By the end of the month, Yugoslavia was firmly in German hands and mainland Greece had fallen, forcing the British to evacuate the units sent to aid their Balkan allies.

But the campaign was not quite over, particularly for the Luftwaffe. As early as 15 April, General Alexander Lohr, commanding *Luftflotte 4*, had suggested that the vitally important island of Crete, which dominated routes in the eastern Mediterranean, should be seized by paratroop and air-landing assault regiments belonging to the Luftwaffe. After hasty consultations with Mussolini, Hitler agreed, initiating the first (and so far the only) strategic use of airborne forces. General Kurt Student's

Fliegerkorps XI, comprising an air-landing assault regiment of four battalions, three parachute regiments and an air-landing division, was immediately made ready to carry out Operation *Merkur* ('Mercury'). Some problems arose – the air-landing division did not arrive in time and had to be replaced at the last moment by the 5th Mountain Division – but by 20 May the Luftwaffe had amassed over 700 Ju 52s and 80 gliders, supported by 650 fighters, bombers and reconnaissance machines.

High casualties on Crete

The initial glider and parachute landings on 20 May suffered high casualties and it was only through a mixture of tough fighting and British miscalculations that airfields at Maleme, Canea and Heraklion were finally secured. British survivors were evacuated 10 days later; in the process the Luftwaffe imposed heavy casualties on the Royal Navy, sinking three cruisers and six destroyers in a major air-sea campaign. But the capture of Crete was costly. By 1 June, the German airborne troops had suffered 5140 casualties out of a committed force of 13,000, while the Luftwaffe had lost 220 aircraft, including the rather sobering total of 119 Ju 52s, the destruction of which left the transport squadrons sorely depleted. It was a high price to pay, especially so close to 'Barbarossa'.

Many of the Luftwaffe units involved in the Balkans had less than three weeks in which to redeploy for 'Barbarossa'. They joined formations stretching from the Baltic coast to Hungary and Romania, divided into three luftflotten, each assigned to support an Army Group in the forthcoming assault. In the north, *Luftflotte 1* (commanded by General Keller) deployed 430 combat aircraft and about 50 transports as part of Field Marshal Ritter von Leeb's Army Group North, the main objective of which was the city of Leningrad. As they advanced, they would make contact with Finnish troops attacking out of Karelia, who were backed by 60 Luftwaffe aircraft under Colonel Neilsen. *Luftflotte 2* (under Kesselring) had 980 combat aircraft and 90 transports, reflecting its support for Field Marshal Fedor von Bock's Army Group Centre, tasked with an attack through Minsk and Smolensk to threaten Moscow. Finally, *Luftflotte 4* (still under Lohr) had 600 combat aircraft and 90 transports with which to support Field Marshal Gerd von Rundstedt's Army Group South, aiming for Kiev and Kharkov to secure the Ukraine.

The attack on Russia began early on 22 June. As always, the primary Luftwaffe task was the seizure of air superiority. Despite the disparity of numbers when compared to the Soviet Air Force, the operation was a remarkable success. Airfields had been identified

Left: Men of the 5th Mountain Division wait to board the Junkers Ju 52 transports that will carry them to reinforce the parachute and glider landings on Crete, May 1941. The division took part in Operation 'Mercury' at short notice, but was relatively easy to adapt to the role of airborne infantry.

Right: The costs of Operation 'Mercury' were high: German airborne troops suffered 5140 casualties out of a committed force of 13,000. Here, the twisted bodies of men killed in a badly landed DFS 230 glider await the burial parties. Losses such as these were difficult to replace.

Below: German paratroopers climb aboard the Junkers Ju 52 transport that will carry them to Crete, May 1941. The distinctive paratrooper's helmet is well illustrated, while the Feldwebel (Sergeant) in the centre shows his rank insignia clearly. Paratroopers such as these were all members of the Luftwaffe.

by high-altitude reconnaissance machines in the weeks leading up to the campaign, enabling Luftwaffe units on 22 June to aim for precise targets. The results were dramatic. An estimated 1800 Soviet aircraft were lost on the first day; by 29 June the Luftwaffe High Command was claiming (correctly, as it turned out) to have destroyed over 4000 enemy machines, all for a loss to themselves of about 150 frontline aircraft. *Luftflotte 2* alone claimed 2500 Soviet aircraft in the first week.

Overall air superiority was not possible – with a frontline stretching nearly 1600km (1000 miles) from north to south, there were always going to be gaps – and many Soviet pilots lived to fight on with replacement aircraft, but the success of the pre-emptive

strikes did mean that Luftwaffe units could shift to support of ground units almost straight away. Aircraft such as the Bf 110 and Ju 87, which had proved vulnerable during the Battle of Britain, suddenly found that they could fly with impunity, and it was these aircraft, together with Hs 123s, that became familiar sights over the battlefield. Unlike in earlier campaigns, where the emphasis had been on interdiction, hitting troop concentrations and communications targets to weaken the enemy's frontline capability, the Luftwaffe soon discovered that it could have a more immediate effect by attacking enemy forces on the frontline itself. In many ways, they had no choice. Army commanders, now fighting their fifth major campaign in 21 months, had grown used to the fruits of air superiority and their demands for close support were legion, while many of the traditional 'indirect' targets, such as roads and railways, were less vital in the relatively primitive society of the Soviet Union. By late June, about 60 per cent of all air sorties were being flown in 'direct' support of the army groups.

Air-to-ground sorties

As with the pre-emptive strikes, the results were dramatic. In the north, where von Leeb's men advanced swiftly through the Baltic States to approach Leningrad, the emphasis was more on transport than ground strafing – both Ju 52s and Ju 88s were used to airlift fuel to the armoured spearheads – but elsewhere, it was the Soviet Army that took the full force of Luftwaffe attacks. In Army Group Centre, Guderian's Panzer Group 2 depended on Ju 87s to dive-bomb them across the River Bug and into Brest-Litovsk.

Above: General Hans Jurgen Stumpff (saluting), the commander of Luftflotte 5 in Norway, inspects Luftwaffe personnel who are about to be deployed to the East for 'Barbarossa', June 1941. The men can have no idea of the nightmare that will ensue.

Right: Fitters work on specialised equipment in the nose section of a Dornier Do 17P long-range reconnaissance aircraft before its flight over the Soviet Union in 1941. The Do 17P was designed specifically for such tasks; during Operation 'Barbarossa', enemy airfields and supply dumps were particular priorities.

Below: General Alexander Lohr (centre), the commander of Luftflotte 4 in support of von Rundstedt's Army Group South during 'Barbarossa', briefs General Hans Jeschonnek (right), Luftwaffe Chief of Staff. The problems with the Luftwaffe led to the suicide of Jeschonnek in August 1943.

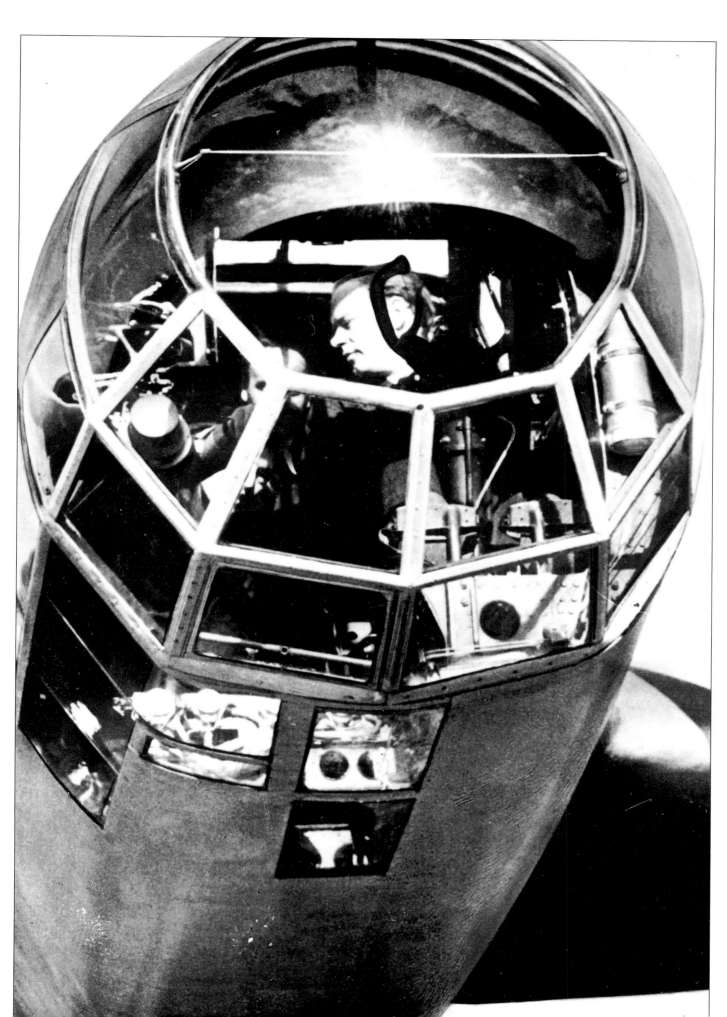

Above: Hitting Soviet supply lines was a major task of the Stukas during Operation 'Barbarossa'. Here, a bomb explodes close to a pontoon bridge across the River Dnieper, the main bridge having been destroyed already. Note the Stuka peeling away in the top right-hand corner of the photograph.

Right: The destruction of Soviet railways was another way of cutting off supplies to frontline units. This photograph shows the aftermath of a Luftwaffe bombing raid on a railway-yard in the Ukraine in 1941: storage sheds have been burnt out and vehicles wrecked. There is not much left.

Below: A Junkers Ju 87 Stuka is photographed in the aftermath of a dive-bombing attack – note the shackle for the centre-line bomb hanging free. Although the Stuka was dangerously slow and vulnerable when it encountered enemy fighters, it was still a formidable weapon against unprotected ground forces. It would continue in use until 1945.

Afterwards, Luftwaffe aircraft of all descriptions were used to ensure that the massive encirclements around Minsk and Smolensk did not develop 'leaks', bombing Soviet units that tried to escape and smashing attempted counterattacks before they could materialise. Similar actions in the south enabled von Rundstedt to thrust deep into the Ukraine, culminating in September in the giant encirclement around Kiev, aided by

Guerian's panzers diverted south from Smolensk. The Kiev 'pocket' contained more than 665,000 Soviet soldiers, as well as 884 tanks and nearly 4000 artillery pieces, all of them captured.

Meanwhile, the Luftwaffe had been carrying out interdiction missions, and though these were not as frequent as in previous campaigns, they did have an impact. Ju 88s, He 111s and Do 17s ranged far and wide behind Soviet lines, seeking out rail targets, bridges and supply depots. Hitler had insisted that they did not try to destroy Soviet industry – he realised that it was dispersed and hard to find, and was fully aware that the diversion of effort involved would weaken airpower elsewhere – but the record of success against other targets was high. *Fliegerkorps II*, part of Kesselring's *Luftflotte 2*, for example, destroyed 356 trains, 14 bridges and innumerable troop concentrations between 22 June

and 9 September 1941, and its achievement was by no means unique. As early as 9 July, it was reported that rail traffic to the west of the River Dnieper was at a standstill, paralysing any Soviet attempts to recover the initiative.

In the light of these successes, the enormous advances made by German forces between June and October 1941 came as no surprise. In the north, Leningrad was effectively besieged by late September; in the centre, Smolensk was captured before Hitler made the decision to divert Guderian south to effect the encirclement of Kiev; in the south, after Kiev von Rundstedt advanced to seize Kharkov and (temporarily) Rostov. It looked as if 'Barbarossa' would work.

Above: German troops advance past the burning outskirts of a Soviet industrial complex, summer 1941. Although the fires in the background could have been started by Luftwaffe bombers, it is equally possible that they were the work of retreating Soviet forces, intent on a policy of 'scorched earth'.

Opposite above: Waffen-SS troops cross a Russian river, summer 1941. The destroyed bridge has interrupted enemy resupply, but it is now delaying the German advance.

Opposite below: A Fieseler Fi 156 Storch light observation aircraft uses a road as its landing strip, Ukraine, summer 1941.

But things started to go wrong in early October, just as Guderian and the other elements of Army Group Centre were advancing on Moscow. Massive encirclements were carried out around Vyazma and Bryansk, yielding a further 673,000 prisoners, but by the end of the month the advance had foundered in a sea of mud as the autumn rains began. Panzers suddenly found that they could not move, and Luftwaffe squadrons fared no better, having to cope with airstrips that simply disappeared overnight. A sharp frost hardened the ground in early November, sufficient to allow the panzers to advance to within 30km (19 miles) of Moscow, but as the temperatures dropped to as low as minus 22 degrees Fahrenheit and snow storms swept the front, a whole series of new problems emerged. Luftwaffe ground crews found that they could not start aircraft engines – oil simply froze solid – and even when sorties could be flown, recognition of ground targets often proved impossible. By early December, even Hitler had to admit that further progress was unlikely. The campaign was closed down for the winter, just as the Soviets, more used to the conditions, mounted furious counterattacks around their capital. The Luftwaffe could do little to prevent a German withdrawal. It would be a long, hard winter.

Above: A Junkers Ju 88A runs up its engines on an airfield in the Soviet Union, 1941. With a maximum speed of 467kmph (292mph) and operational range of more than 1600km (1000 miles), the Ju 88 was a useful medium bomber, but its bomb-carrying capacity was limited to 1818kg (4000lb).

Below: A Dornier Do 17S high-speed reconnaissance aircraft. The Do 17S was powered by two Daimler-Benz DB 600G liquid-cooled engines, but did not enter squadron service. The engines were diverted to the fighter programme, leaving subsequent Do 17s to make do with BMW-Bramo 323 radials.

Above: A mechanic works on a Messerschmitt Bf 109G/R2 of Jagdgeschwader 3 'Udet', used on the Eastern Front for ground support tasks. The 'bump' on the forward fuselage houses the breech-block of a 13mm Maschinengewehr (MG) 131.

Nevertheless, the Luftwaffe could look back on the five months of campaigning in the Soviet Union with some pride. Fielding an average of only 1400 serviceable combat aircraft at any time, Luftwaffe units had managed to fly over 180,000 sorties under a wide range of geographic and climatic conditions. In the process, they had destroyed at least 15,500 enemy aircraft, 3200 tanks, 57,600 vehicles, 2450 artillery pieces and 1200 locomotives, while making a major contribution to the advance of ground formations. Nor were the costs excessively high – altogether, 2093 aircraft were lost (a fair proportion to accidents rather than enemy action) – and losses could be replaced. Indeed, on 27 December 1941, the Luftwaffe as a whole could still field 1332 level-bombers, 1472 fighters and 326 dive-bombers – a formidable force by any reckoning (one disconcerting aspect of the Russian campaign from the Luftwaffe's point of view was the high loses suffered by German air units during ground-attack missions, when Russian troops tended to stand firm and open fire with everything to hand, rather than scatter and seek any cover available – aircraft were invariably always hit).

But the fact that 'Barbarossa' had not led to the promised collapse of the Soviet Union, necessitating new campaigns in 1942, was worrying, particularly when operations were still continuing in the West and the Mediterranean. By the end of 1941, pilots and crews were tired, the introduction of new aircraft designs had been delayed and the Luftwaffe was in desperate need of time in which to rest and refit. That time was not available.

Above: *Ground crew manhandle a Junkers Ju 88A on an airfield in the Soviet Union that is beginning to show the effects of the autumn rains, 1941.*

Left: *Junkers Ju 88As fly towards their allotted targets, Eastern Front 1941. During the early stages of 'Barbarossa' the Luftwaffe encountered little aerial opposition.*

Below: *A fully laden Junkers Ju 87 Stuka taxies out for take-off, Eastern Front, winter 1941-42. The frozen ground could be exploited to create airstrips, but the low temperatures of a Russian winter played havoc in other ways, not least when engine oil froze. Special heat generators had to be used to keep engines operable, but at least take-offs and landings were relatively trouble-free.*

CHAPTER 7

THE FALTERING GRIP – RUSSIA 1942-43

During the Stalingrad and Kursk battles the Luftwaffe suffered horrendous losses in both aircraft and crews. New aircraft were slow coming into service, and the Soviet Air Force was growing in strength and effectiveness.

Left: Smoke pouring from its port engine, a Henschel Hs 129 makes its final dive. The Hs 129 was a purpose-built ground-attack and anti-tank aircraft, heavily armed and armoured.

Above: A pre-production Heinkel He 177A Greif (Griffin) heavy bomber. The He 177 was a big disappointment to the Luftwaffe, taking from 1939 until late 1942 to enter squadron service.

The winter of 1941-42 on the Eastern Front was exceptionally harsh for those German soldiers and airmen called upon to endure it. Not only were the physical conditions worse than anyone had expected – temperatures as low as minus 20 degrees Fahrenheit invariably felt colder because of the icy winds blowing

from Siberia – but the Soviets soon proved that they could adapt much more readily than their enemies. The counterattacks around Moscow, which began in early December 1941, may have led to heavy Soviet casualties, but individual Russian soldiers did not seem to be affected by the weather.

Above: The desolation of a winter airfield on the Eastern Front is clearly indicated in this photograph of Junkers Ju-87D Stukas. The snowdrifts and poor visibility make operational flying impossible; all that can be done is to protect the aircraft from the elements and wait for better times.

Right: A Junkers Ju 52 transport flies over the snowy wastes of the Russian Steppes, winter 1942-43. It was aircraft such as this that tried in vain to keep the encircled soldiers at Stalingrad supplied with essentials. However, the Ju 52 was too slow and vulnerable to survive in a hostile air environment.

Above left: Junkers Ju 88A medium bombers on a frozen airfield on the Eastern Front, winter 1942-43. The ground has been swept to produce a runway, but the cold has necessitated covering the engines with tarpaulins. The machine gun mounted to the rear of the cockpit implies that an operation is imminent.

Below left: With temperatures so low on the Eastern Front that engine oil could freeze solid, methods had to be found to keep aircraft flying. Here, heaters have been mounted around the engines of a Ju 88A, while all Perspex surfaces have been covered.

Above: An Arado Ar 196A reconnaissance and coastal patrol floatplane prepares for take-off, 1942. This particular aircraft probably belongs to See Aufklärungsgruppe 131, *based in Norway. Its task is to locate Allied convoys.*

It took until February 1942 for the attacks to be contained. By then, two German strongholds had been surrounded, one at Demyansk and the other at Kholm, both to the northwest of Moscow. Göring was given the task of keeping the isolated pockets resupplied by air and, against the odds, he succeeded. At Demyansk, about 100,000 men belonging to the Sixteenth Army had been cut off. Starting on 20 February, Ju 52s drawn from all theatres (including training establishments in Germany) flew as many missions as they could to deliver supplies sufficient to keep the soldiers alive. Despite having to fly 160km (100 miles) over Soviet-occupied territory, the fleet of nearly 600 Ju 52s managed to deliver about 305 tonnes (300 tons) of supplies a day, meeting little opposition from an enemy air force that was still reeling from the attacks of the previous June. The siege was lifted by ground troops on 18 May, at about the same time as the much smaller Kholm pocket was also relieved. It had contained about 3500 men and supplies were air-dropped or, in an emergency, delivered by one-way glider missions using DFS 230s and Gotha Go 242s. In both cases, Demyansk and Kholm, Luftwaffe aircrews had carried out a dangerous and difficult task, but their success was soon to

return to haunt them. The loss of nearly 300 Ju 52s meant that multi-engine pilot training had to be curtailed; more crucially, Hitler now believed that surrounded armies could be kept supplied by air, regardless of the circumstances.

The Luftwaffe in the Crimea

Once the spring thaw began in April 1942, German planners turned their attention to the next campaign. Hitler had already decided that the priority lay in the southern sector of the Eastern Front, calling for an advance to the River Don to shield the flank of a major attack into the oil-rich Caucasus, to be codenamed Operation *Blau* ('Blue'). However, before that could be carried out, the front as a whole needed to be stabilised. In May, attacks were carried out in the north to eliminate Soviet-held salients, while farther south the Crimea had to be cleared. The Luftwaffe

Above: *A Dornier Do 24T air-sea rescue and transport flying boat is brought ashore for maintenance in a harbour in northern Norway, 1942. They also tracked Allied convoys.*

Below: *A Heinkel He 111H-6 is loaded with practice LT F5b torpedoes, the aim being to create a medium bomber that could be used against Allied convoys in the Arctic.*

was called upon to support all such operations, devoting more and more of its effort to close support rather than its pre-war preference for longer-range interdiction. Air superiority could never be guaranteed, but by concentrating resources in key sectors, the Luftwaffe could still overwhelm the enemy. This was shown to good effect in the Crimea, where von Richthofen's *Fliegerkorps VIII* made a decisive contribution to the seizure of Sevastopol, dropping more than 20,321 tonnes (20,000 tons) of bombs and destroying 140 Soviet aircraft between 2 June and 4 July.

By then, Operation 'Blue' had begun, but the Luftwaffe was finding it increasingly difficult to provide the aircraft and aircrews needed, particularly now that campaigns were being fought in so many different locations. Indeed, one more unforeseen duty was the Luftwaffe's contribution to the naval war, as units were transferred to Norway to carry out attacks on Allied convoys shipping supplies to Murmansk and Archangel. By June 1942, over 100 Ju

Right: Hermann Graf, photographed as a major wearing the Knight's Cross of the Iron Cross with Oakleaves and Swords in 1942. Graf was awarded the Oakleaves on 17 May 1942, by which time he had downed 104 enemy aircraft. Note the Operational Flying Clasp above his left pocket.

Below: A pair of Messerschmitt Bf 109F fighters fly over the Eastern Front, summer 1943. By this stage, the Bf 109F is beginning to show its age; although still a capable fighter, particularly in the hands of men like Hartmann, it is now encountering superior Soviet machines. After 1942, the dominant version of the Bf 109 was the 109G, which made up over 70 per cent of the total received by the Luftwaffe. Though heavily armed and equipped, the 'Gustav' was not as good a machine as the lighter E and F versions.

Pages 102-103: A Heinkel He 111H, possibly of Kampfgeschwader 4 'General Wever', is heavily camouflaged against surprise Soviet air attack, 1943. Once air superiority could no longer be guaranteed, aircraft had to be dispersed and carefully disguised while on the ground. It curtailed operational freedom and response times.

88s and 40 torpedo-carrying He 111s, plus Ju 87s, Fw 200s and Blohm und Voss Bv 138 seaplanes, had been devoted to the task of interdicting the convoys, with some success. In May 1942 Convoy PQ16 was badly hit, losing seven merchant ships; two months, later the ill-fated Convoy PQ17 lost 24 out of its total of 34 merchantmen, seven of them to air attack alone. It was a good return on the Luftwaffe's investment, but it meant that even fewer aircraft were available on the Eastern Front.

The drive to Stalingrad

When 'Blue' began on 28 June, therefore, Göring's units were stretched. Squadrons were stripped from elsewhere on the Eastern Front to create a respectable force of nearly 1600 bombers and fighters, but there were few reserves and many of the crews, fresh from Demyansk, Kholm and the Crimea, were desperately tired. Even so, the initial German attacks enjoyed success, not least because the Luftwaffe was constantly on call to ground forces which now expected close support at the drop of a hat. The roles carried out were the familiar ones of creating and maintaining air superiority over the battlefield, enabling bombers and dive-bombers to locate and hit enemy force targets. By 6 July, Army Group South had crossed the Don opposite Voronezh, encircling and destroying most of the Soviet forces to the west of the river. The Germans should then have halted and transferred the bulk of their effort to take Rostov and push into the Caucasus. Unfortunately, Hitler intervened, splitting Army Group South into Army Groups A and B, with the former moving into the Caucasus while the latter advanced south along the Don to mask a perceived Soviet build-up around Stalingrad. The situation was

Above: A Heinkel He 111H of Kampfgeschwader 53 'Legion Condor' waits to be bombed-up, Leningrad Front, spring 1943. The aircraft is parked on a specially created packed-earth standing, probably to avoid mud.

Above left: A Junkers Ju 52 hospital transport is off-loaded, summer 1943. Casualty evacuation was a major task for the Ju 52s, particularly on the Eastern Front where vast distances made any alternative process too lengthy for the wounded.

Below left: Lightly wounded soldiers wait to board a Junkers Ju 52 hospital transport, Eastern Front, summer 1943. Red Cross markings are an attempt to gain immunity from attack, though there are no guarantees that the Soviets will honour such niceties.

made worse on 30 July when Hitler intervened again, this time to insist that Army Group B, spearheaded by the Fourth Panzer and Sixth Armies, had to capture rather than merely mask the city of Stalingrad. It was a fatal decision: instead of a concerted attack with a single operational aim, the Germans were now split, trying to carry out two diverging advances which stretched available resources to breaking point.

The Luftwaffe stretched to the limits

This was keenly felt by the Luftwaffe, the local strength of which had declined to little more than 1300 aircraft by mid-July. The crews of these machines were now expected to maintain the existing levels of close support over a frontline that was over 4320km (2700 miles) long, while also satisfying Hitler's additional call for

raids on Soviet supply lines as far away as Astrakhan on the Caspian Sea. Some success was achieved – by 9 August elements of Army Group A, with Luftwaffe support, had pushed nearly 320km (200 miles) into the Caucasus, while two weeks later, also with air backing, General Friedrich Paulus' Sixth Army reached the River Volga to the north of Stalingrad – but it could not last. As aircraft were lost to enemy action and, more often at this stage, to operational accident, they were not replaced quickly enough, while lack of maintenance facilities and airbases meant that quite simple repairs were taking far too long to effect. In addition, Luftwaffe crews were being asked to do too much, often flying four or five missions a day against an enemy who was gradually recovering air strength both from his own industrial output (from factories safely ensconced beyond the Ural Mountains) and from Anglo-American aid convoys. The balance was beginning to shift.

Attempts to relieve Stalingrad

This was made apparent as the Battle for Stalingrad developed. As Paulus tried to take the city in September 1942, his forces were held, despite herculean efforts by available Luftwaffe squadrons. The battle degenerated into a nightmare of urban fighting, to which the Luftwaffe could contribute little: enemy positions were just too close to German lines and too much bombing merely produced additional rubble for Soviet infantrymen to hide in. By October, Paulus was firmly fixed in place; a month later the Soviets struck his weakly held flanks and, in a brilliant manoeuvre, surrounded him in the city. Nearly 300,000 German troops occupied a pocket that measured 48 square kilometres (30 square

miles), just as the winter weather closed in. Hitler refused to sanction a breakout, even when a German counterattack from outside the city got to within 56km (35 miles) of the trapped men. Instead, remembering the successes at Demyansk and Kholm, he ordered Göring to keep Paulus supplied by air (the head of the Luftwaffe had assured Hitler that his air force could supply the trapped Sixth Army at Stalingrad).

Stalingrad – the impossible task

It was an impossible task. Paulus' army required an estimated 762 tonnes (750 tons) of supplies a day if it was to survive as a fighting force, and even when this figure was reduced to 508 tonnes (500 tons) just to ensure bare survival (which included the slaughter of all the horses and their carcasses issued as part of the meat ration), it was way beyond Luftwaffe capability to satisfy. A Ju 52 could carry about two tonnes (two tons) of supplies in a single mission, but the apparently simple arithmetic of providing between 375 and 250 aircraft did not work in practical terms. Most transport units on the Eastern Front found it difficult to maintain more than 35 per cent operational capability in the winter months. Thus, although *Fliegerkorps VIII*, given the unenviable task of coordinating the airlift, initially fielded 320 Ju 52s, so few of them were fully serviceable that von Richthofen had to use converted He 111s and any other large aircraft that happened to be available. These included Fw 200s, Junkers Ju 90s and 290s and Heinkel He 177s, few of which proved suitable for transport tasks and none of which survived the winter conditions. Moreover, as the airlift progressed, Soviet ground attacks gradually pushed German airbases

Left: *An Arado Ar 232B-0 four-engined general purpose transport aircraft, 1943. Only four such aircraft were built, seeing service in the Ergänzungs-Transport Gruppe (Replacement Transport Wing) in Russia in 1943-44, where they seem to have been involved in clandestine operations.*

Right: *A Junkers Ju 52 comes in to land on a grass airstrip on the Eastern Front, summer 1943. The immense flatness of the Steppes can be appreciated; such terrain seemed endless to those who fought over it and aircraft were often the only way of ensuring fast movement.*

Below: *Men of a German cyclist unit deplane from a Junkers Ju 52 transport, Eastern Front 1943. Such a combination of air transportation and pedal-power was one answer to the vast open spaces of Russia, but both means of movement were potentially very vulnerable to Soviet weapons.*

Above: By 1943, after enormous losses in the East, Germany is beginning to run short of manpower and is spreading its recruitment into the occupied countries of Western Europe. These are Flemish volunteers in SS uniform with Luftwaffe helmets.

Below: A Heinkel He 111H bomber on an airfield on the Eastern Front, 1943. The proximity of the bomb-dump implies that the aircraft is about to be loaded before an operation. Without fighter protection, the He 111 was very vulnerable.

farther away from Stalingrad, so that by early January 1943 some of the transports were having to fly round trips of nearly 800km (500 miles) in appalling conditions against a rapidly recovering Soviet Air Force. On a good day, the Luftwaffe managed to deliver 304 tonnes (300 tons), but the average was nearer 203 tonnes (200 tons), and on some days nothing at all could be carried. It was clearly not enough.

A supreme effort wasted

Meanwhile, Paulus' men suffered from constant Soviet attacks in addition to the cold and starvation. On 16 January they lost control of the airfield at Pitomnik inside the pocket, leaving the much smaller strip at Gumrak as the only location where transports could land. When that too fell on 21 January, there was little the Luftwaffe could continue to do. Some supplies were parachuted in, but the pocket was by then so small that most of the canisters fell behind Soviet lines. On 31 January 1943, Paulus surrendered

Below: A Henschel Hs 129 close-support aircraft, photographed post-war while being evaluated by the United States Army Air Force – hence the rather spurious fuselage markings. Some Hs 129s were fitted with a 75mm anti-tank cannon.

the remnants of his army; isolated groups held out for a further 48 hours. The airlift therefore lasted officially for 70 days (25 November 1942 to 2 February 1943), during which 3500 transport sorties had managed to deliver just over 6604 tonnes (6500 tons) of supplies and evacuate about 34,000 wounded. The cost to the Luftwaffe was crippling. *Fliegerkorps VIII* lost a total of 488 aircraft, of which 266 were Ju 52s.

Numbers begin to tell

Even before Paulus surrendered, Soviet armies were taking the opportunity to advance, pushing other German forces back beyond Kharkov. Counterattacks managed to stabilise the situation for the Germans by March, but for the first time Luftwaffe support could not be guaranteed. The losses of the winter had not been fully replaced and conditions on the ground were so bad, particularly during the spring thaw, that airbases were incapable of sustaining the squadrons. More worryingly, the Soviet Air Force was beginning to impose itself on the battlefield, fielding new and much more effective aircraft in potentially overwhelming numbers. One of the results was that the Ju 87, upon which so much of the close air support depended, became extremely vulnerable. As had been shown during the Battle of Britain, a slow-moving,

Above: Luftwaffe General Gunther Korten replaced Jeschonnek as Chief of Staff after the latter's suicide in August 1943. Korten, like his predecessor, found Göring impossible to work for.

Below: A Junkers Ju 87G, equipped with a 37mm Flak 18 cannon under its starboard wing. The decision to fit Stukas with cannon for anti-tank purposes was made in 1942.

obsolescent dive-bomber could not survive for long in an air environment dominated by fast interceptor fighters. This was not helped by the fact that the replacement for the Stuka had been delayed – the Henschel Hs 129B had still to be proved in battle – just at a time when the Soviets were perfecting their ground-attack techniques using the purpose-built Ilyushin Il-2 *Shturmovik*.

The Luftwaffe at Kursk

The gradually shifting balance of air capability on the Eastern Front was shown during Operation *Zitadelle* ('Citadel'), when Hitler ordered two of his armies, the Ninth and Fourth Panzer, to attack both flanks of a salient jutting into German lines around the city of Kursk. If this had been done when the salient first materialised in March 1943, the chances of victory might have been good, but the Germans were in no condition to carry out a hasty offensive. Ground forces needed to be re-equipped (not least with the new Panther and Tiger tanks), and the Luftwaffe was crying out for time to refit. The offensive did not begin, therefore, until 5 July, giving the Soviets ample time in which to prepare formidable defences.

As it was, Hitler had managed to amass a considerable force of over 900,000 men, 10,000 guns and 2700 armoured fighting vehicles. Supporting them were 1800 Luftwaffe combat aircraft: *Luftflotte IV* had 1100 machines in the south, backing Fourth Panzer Army, while *Fliegerdivision 1* fielded 700 in the north, supporting Ninth Army. And the Luftwaffe brought a new aircraft to the battle: the Henschel 129B tank-buster. Organised into a unit commanded by Hauptmann Bruno Meyer, the Hs 129Bs showed themselves to be very effective against Soviet tanks, their tungsten-cored 30mm shells stopping a Russian armoured brigade and forcing it to retreat on 9 July.

It was not enough. Despite heavy Luftwaffe commitment (some pilots were flying six or seven sorties a day during the first week of the battle), the Soviet defences proved to be a trap, enmeshing ground forces in line after line of well-laid defences.

After the battle the Soviets resumed their offensives, and the Luftwaffe was forced to provide air support for ground units as the Germans desperately tried to reform its defensive lines. This was achieved, but in the process the Luftwaffe started to run short of fuel. By 23 July the Germans were back at their start positions.

Following the failure of the Kursk offensive the Luftwaffe concentrated the majority of its strength in support of army units trying to hold the line of the River Donetz. However, the air force was overstretched, and units had to be switched from one end of the line to the other in response to Russian moves. An inevitable result was that Soviet territorial gains in late 1943 were substantial, pushing the Germans back beyond the Dnieper River, little more than 320km (200 miles) from the pre-war border. If this had been the only battleground, the Germans might yet have recovered, but by the end of 1943 the strategic nightmare of war on more than one front simultaneously had become reality. Many fighter squadrons were being withdrawn to defend German skies against the Allied bombers.

Right: As Russian troops advance against German positions in the summer of 1943, they undergo artillery and air attack. The soldier in the foreground has just been hit by shrapnel.

Below: A well camouflaged German 75mm Pak 40 anti-tank gun at Kursk. Overhead, the Luftwaffe hammers Soviet positions mercilessly to try to breach the Russian defences.

DEFENDING THE REICH'S SKIES

The Allied bombing campaign against Germany began fitfully, but once it had gained momentum the Luftwaffe was unable to prevent the wholesale destruction of the Third Reich's cities and industry.

Left: *An RAF Avro Lancaster bomber, one of 288, is caught on camera during a daylight raid on oil-storage depots at Bec-d'Ambes and Pauillac near Bordeaux, 4 August 1944.*

Above: *Focke-Wulf Fw 190A fighters taxi for take-off on a fairly rudimentary airfield, 1943. The Fw 190, first flown in June 1939, began to reach frontline squadrons in mid-1941.*

Until 1942, the need to devote large numbers of fighters or even anti-aircraft (flak) guns to the defence of Germany had seemed unnecessary. The air raids mounted by RAF Bomber Command in 1940 and 1941 were spasmodic and, in most cases, inflicted little damage; indeed, such had been the success of exist-

ing German air defences against them that the British had shifted from daylight to night-time attacks, with inevitable effects on navigation and bomb-aiming accuracy. By August 1941, the British themselves were forced to admit that, of the aircraft flying against the German industrial Ruhr, only about a third were dropping

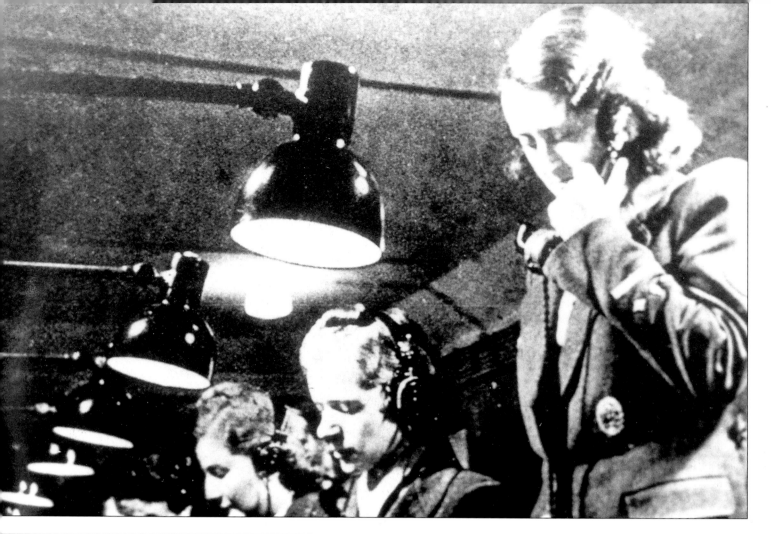

Above: A Hauptgruppenführerin *(as denoted by the three stars and single bar on her sleeve) of the* Luftwaffenhelferinnenschaft *helps to coordinate air defences, 1941. She is in charge of the female telephonists, who are in contact with night-fighter airfields and anti-aircraft sites.*

Left: A battery of 128mm Flugabwehrkanone *(Flak)* 40 *anti-aircraft guns prepares for action in Germany, 1942. Designed and tested in 1937, the Flak 40 could project a 26kg (57lb) shell to a maximum vertical ceiling of 14,800m (nine miles), giving it a formidable capability against Allied bombers.*

Above right: A Flakwaffenhelferin *gun-layer checks the elevation of a heavy anti-aircraft weapon, 1944. Volunteers from the* Luftwaffenhelferinnen *were used from October 1943 to bolster German air-defence units, releasing men for frontline service.*

Centre right: An Oberhelferin *(denoted by the two chevrons on her left sleeve) of the* Flakwaffenhelferinnen *works the elevator wheel on the side of a heavy anti-aircraft gun, 1944. Female volunteers never served outside Germany.*

Below right: The Waffen-SS crew of a 20mm Flak 38 *quadruple-barrelled light anti-aircraft gun display their skills to a visiting Luftwaffe officer.*

bombs within 8km (five miles) of their designated targets. At a time when German forces elsewhere were seizing the Balkans and thrusting deep into the Soviet Union, there appeared to be little need to boost domestic air defence.

This was indicated by the number of air-defence aircraft maintained in Germany: by the end of 1940 a mere 165, increasing to just over 300 a year later. But it would be wrong to dismiss air-defence efforts entirely during this period. As early as July 1940, General Josef Kammhuber was appointed by Göring to develop night defences, and his innovations laid strong foundations for the future. His system became known, logically enough, as the Kammhuber Line, stretching eventually from Denmark to southern France. At its centre was an arrangement nicknamed *Himmelbett* (four-poster bed), whereby the likely approach routes from Britain to the heart of Germany were divided into 'boxes', each of which was defended by a mixture of radar, fighter aircraft, searchlights and flak guns. *Freya* long-range radars were positioned to pick up signs of an incoming raid; as soon as the bombers approached, they would be tracked by a shorter-range *Wurzburg*, linked to night-fighter ground controllers. They would guide individual aircraft in the direction of the bombers, leaving it up to the pilots to intercept by means of visual identification. If this proved impossible, the night-fighters would follow the bombers into the illumination of the searchlight zone; if that failed, the flak guns closer to the targets would come into play. For the time, it was remarkably sophisticated.

Luftwaffe retaliatory raids

In early 1942, however, the RAF improved its capability. The first of its heavy four-engined bombers were deployed and, under the single-minded leadership of Air Marshal Arthur Harris, a new strategy was perfected, based on 'area bombing', whereby entire cities rather than just the factories within them were targeted. This reduced the need for high accuracy but also increased the levels of civilian destruction. On 28/29 March 1942, for example, the city of Lübeck was razed, followed almost a month later by Rostock. In both cases, the bombers flew in a continuous stream, swamping the Kammhuber Line.

Hitler was livid. In the immediate aftermath of the Lübeck raid he ordered *Luftflotte III* to mount retaliatory attacks on Britain. The first occurred on the night of 23/24 April, when 45 Dornier Do 217s hit Exeter, followed by a second raid the following night against the same target. Bath was raided on the very night that the RAF was hitting Rostock, and it was this incident that caused Hitler, in an impassioned speech to the German people, to wave a copy of the pre-war Baedeker Guide to Britain and announce that the cities listed within it would be wiped out one by one. Between then and the end of July, in what became known as the 'Baedeker Raids', Luftwaffe bombers ranged far and wide over England, attacking cities such as Norwich, Exeter, York, Hull and Birmingham. Some of the raids were quite devastating – Exeter was hit for a third time on 3/4 May and set aflame – but *Luftflotte*

Above: In September 1944, Allied airborne troops dropped into southern Holland to seize bridges over the Maas, Waal and Lower Rhine. As part of the 'softening-up' process, the RAF hit the airfield at Arnhem on 16/17 September.

Below: In the aftermath of the RAF raid on the airfield at Arnhem, a Luftwaffe repair and recovery team rests on the wing of a heavily damaged Ju 52. The raid appears to have been successful, although the Ju 52s shown are recoverable.

Above: As part of the same raid on 16/17 September 1944, the Junckers & Co factory at Arnhem was hit. By this stage in the war the RAF had sufficient air superiority to carry out raids such as this with little danger – the Luftwaffe was no longer effective.

Right: Still with the Arnhem raid of 16/17 September 1944, the Luftwaffe repair and recovery team shown opposite has completed its task and the remains of a Ju 52 – the front part of the fuselage and wing-roots – are awaiting collection by the roadside. There is not much of value left.

Below: Another view of the two Junkers Ju 52s heavily damaged at Arnhem, September 1944. All the photographs on these two pages are taken from a roll of film captured by the British in 1944 and developed by Army Intelligence. As far as is known, they have not been published before.

Above: Boeing B-17s of the 381st Bombardment Group, United States 8th Army Air Force create distinctive (and potentially very dangerous) vapour trails as they fly into Germany, 1944. The lead aircraft is a B-17F, with B-17Gs following.

Below: Avro Lancasters of No 463 Squadron RAF Bomber Command fly in formation to carry out a raid over German-occupied Europe, 1944. The Lancaster was designed (and painted) for night-time operations.

Above: *Part of the bomb-load of a Boeing B-17 Flying Fortress bomber begins its descent onto a target in Germany, 1944. The 'dustbin' beneath the fuselage is an H2X radar radome, installed in place of the normal ball turret, indicating that this particular aircraft is a pathfinder.*

Below: *A lead B-17 drops its bombs as a signal for others to do the same, 1944. The aircraft are flying in a loose formation, although their machine guns are still within range of each other to provide mutual defence. The smoke trail in the centre could be a B-17 going down.*

III could not sustain the campaign. Aircraft losses mounted and, with few reserves available, the raids gradually petered out. With the exception of a brief series of attacks on London in early 1944, this was the swansong of the Luftwaffe over the British Isles.

Meanwhile, the RAF had continued to develop, mounting the first of its '1000 Bomber Raids' on 30/31 May 1942 against Cologne. The damage inflicted was not substantial in the light of things to come, but it was indicative of a growing need for German air defences to be improved. Other German cities hit during this time included Hamburg, which was bombed twice by the RAF in July 1942. The city's water supplies and civil defence were smashed in the first raid, while in the second the incendiary bombs dropped by the aircraft caused a multitude of small fires,

Above: *Luftwaffe 'ace' Kurt Buhligen (right) discusses tactics with a fellow pilot, 1944. Buhligen was awarded the Oakleaves on 2 March 1944 after having gained his 96th aerial victory.*

Below: *An experienced pilot briefs newcomers to his squadron on the finer points of fighter techniques. The model in his hand appears to be of a Focke-Wulf Fw 190, with a real one behind.*

Above: Oberstleutnant *(Lieutenant-Colonel) Egon Mayer (centre, in shorts) visits the crash site of one of his daylight 'kills' – a B-17 of the 8th USAAF. Mayer was awarded the Oakleaves to his Knight's Cross (as shown around his neck) on 16 April 1943 after having achieved his 63rd aerial victory. By 1943 the Allied bombing campaign was forcing the Germans to divert aircraft and resources to combat the air threat. The campaign was conducted by both RAF Bomber Command and the US 8th Army Air Force. The Americans hit specific industrial targets while the RAF attacked cities. The latter strategy produced some horrendous casualties. During the raids on Hamburg in July 1943, for example, the firestorm produced destroyed 70 per cent of the city and killed over 30,000 people. It was a foretaste of things to come. Nevertheless, in 1943 the Germans began to organise their defences more effectively to counter the bombing campaign, a combination of the Kammhuber Line and the deployment of more fighters.*

Above right: Oberst *(Colonel) Helmut Lent, one of the most successful Luftwaffe night-fighter 'aces'. He was awarded the Oakleaves to the Knight's Cross (as shown) on 6 June 1942, by which time he had downed a total of 35 night-bombers.*

Centre right: Gordon M Gollob, awarded the Oakleaves to the Knight's Cross on 26 October 1941 for having achieved 85 aerial victories. Gollob replaced Adolf Galland as Inspector General of Fighters on 15 January 1945, by which time he was a major-general.*

Below right: Heinz-Wolfgang Schnaufer, the Luftwaffe's top night-fighter 'ace', credited eventually with 121 kills, mostly RAF Lancaster and Halifax bombers. Known to the RAF as the 'Night Ghost of St Trond' after the name of his base in Belgium, he survived the war.*

Above: The three Focke-Wulf Fw 190A-0s of the manufacturer's flight test line run their engines, summer 1941. In the foreground is a 'small-wing' variant, with two 'large-wing' versions behind. The Fw 190 performed well as a fighter.

which soon linked up and raged unchecked. The resultant fire storm killed thousands, and the RAF returned for a third time on 30 July (though the day before, in response to the local *gauleiter*'s call for all non-essential civilians to leave the city, over one million people had evacuated the city).

A further sign of impending disaster came in August 1942, when the first American bombers began to operate from bases in Britain in large-scale raids. To begin with, the heavily armed B-17 Flying Fortresses and B-24 Liberators confined their daylight raids to targets in occupied France, Belgium and the Netherlands, but their presence threatened a new campaign, forcing the Germans to defend their homeland 24 hours a day. The existing defences would not be able to cope.

The strengthening of German defences

In response, by the end of 1942 Luftwaffe strength in the West had increased to nearly 400 night- and 200 day-fighters, backed by flak units fielding more than 1100 anti-aircraft guns. The effects elsewhere of such reinforcement were significant, for nearly all the aircraft involved had to be drawn from existing formations. Milch made great efforts to increase production, but this would take time to effect and had the added disadvantage of curtailing the development of new designs. By now the war was in its fourth year, yet the Luftwaffe was still equipped with aircraft types that had been in frontline service when the conflict began. Some, like the Bf 109

and Ju 88, had been, and would continue to be, refined in terms of speed, armament and endurance, but others, particularly the Bf 110 and Ju 87, were already dangerously obsolete. Their planned replacements – most notably the Heinkel He 177 bomber and Messerschmitt Me 210 long-range fighter – had suffered from lack of development funding and their introduction had been seriously delayed. Even when they did enter squadron service, their teething troubles were such that their impact was significantly less than expected.

Anti-bomber tactics

In such circumstances, it is remarkable just how effective German air defence became in 1943 and early 1944. At a time when Allied raids were becoming more sophisticated – the RAF, for example, introduced Oboe and H2S precision blind-bombing radar sets to improve accuracy, while the Americans flew in defensive 'box' formations to protect their bombers – the Germans managed to impose considerable casualties by day and night. Once the Americans began to penetrate German airspace in early 1943, hitting U-boat bases and installations, Bf 109s and Fw 190s armed

Above: *Focke-Wulf Fw 190A-4/R6 Pulk-Zerstörer, fitted with two underwing Wfr.Gr.21 aerial mortars. The latter were designed for use against US daylight bombers: that mortar bombs lobbed at them would break up the 'box' formations.*

Below: *A Messerschmitt Bf 109F fighter stands in readiness to intercept American daylight bombers, 1943. The pilot is already on board, waiting for the order to 'scramble', while other pilots, presumably at a lesser state of readiness, relax.*

Above: A Heinkel He 219 V1 Uhu *(Owl) night-fighter, originally flown by* **Nachtjagdgeschwader 1***, on display in Britain after the war. This example is equipped with a FuG 212* **Lichtenstein** *interception radar.*

with 20mm cannon and underwing rockets were used in head-on attacks that broke up the 'box' formations and left individual aircraft vulnerable to destruction. Such techniques culminated in heavy American losses in August and October 1943, when B-17s of the US 8th Army Air Force tried to hit the Messerschmitt works at Regensburg and ball-bearing factories at Schweinfurt. On each occasion, 60 Flying Fortresses failed to return, forcing the Americans to pause to rethink their strategy.

Wild and tame boars

The Luftwaffe response to the RAF's night-time campaign was more complex. The Kammhuber Line was still effective in early 1943, though its destructive capability had been undermined by the British adoption of the bomber stream and was to be further degraded by the use of 'Window' – thin strips of aluminium dropped by the bombers to swamp enemy radars – first used in the devastating fire raids on Hamburg in late July/early August, in which an estimated 50,000 civilians were killed (see above). But Kammhuber's defences could be adapted. One method, suggested and implemented by Major Hajo Hermann (who had also suggested bombing the United States mainland using flying boats, which would be refueled and rearmed by U-boats lying offshore), was for the night-fighters to concentrate over the target rather than

along the approach route, using British marker flares and German searchlights for illumination of enemy bombers. Known as *Wilde Sau* (Wild Boar), this precluded the need for night-fighters to depend on compromised radars to guide them to the bombers; at the same time, it disrupted the bomber stream at just the time when it needed to be concentrated. Wild Boar was not a cure, but at least it provided some cover for German cities while new radar equipment was developed, which would work in the face of 'Window' jamming. A later refinement, nicknamed *Zahme Sau* (Tame Boar), had the night-fighters guided to the bomber stream, as indicated on ground radars by the sudden impact of Window on their screens. Once in contact, they then infiltrated the stream, picking out their targets as and when they could, even if this meant accompanying the RAF back to its bases in England.

Technology also had a part to play. Night-fighters such as the Ju 88 and Bf 110 were equipped with on-board interception radars so that, once guided into the stream, they could track individual bombers without having to worry about interference. The most effective on-board radar was the SN-2 *Lichtenstein*, working on a much lower frequency than the ground-based *Wurzburgs* and therefore less affected by Window, and the array of nose-mounted aerials soon became a distinguishing feature of night-fighter aircraft. Some of those aircraft were also fitted with special upward-firing cannon, known as 'jazz music', which enabled them to position themselves directly beneath a British bomber, out of sight of the aircraft's crew, then rake the aircraft along its entire fuselage, killing the occupants and exploding the fuel tanks. This proved so effective that RAF crews were sometimes told that the Germans were deliberately using anti-aircraft shells that looked like an exploding bomber in order to demoralise them. Few of the crews believed it, although all were aware that flak defences were becoming much more effective.

Defending the skies

As 1943 progressed, Hitler ordered entire flak units back into Germany from other theatres in an attempt to stave off the bombers, concentrating them around key locations, such as the Ruhr and Berlin. This increased the level of defensive fire but also left frontline ground units in the Soviet Union and Italy suddenly bereft of protection. As a proportion of the withdrawn flak units were equipped with the 88mm gun, devastatingly effective in the anti-armour role, the problems grew worse.

Nevertheless, the combination of anti-aircraft fire, searchlights and improved night-fighter tactics imposed horrendous casualties on the attacking night-bombers. During the so-called 'Battle of Berlin' between 18/19 November 1943 and the end of January 1944, for example, the RAF lost 384 aircraft in just 14 raids against the German capital. In addition, on the night of 30/31 March 1944, in a raid against Nuremberg, Bomber Command lost 95 aircraft out of a committed force of 795. It looked as if the air defences had the upper hand.

High attrition rates

But this was a false assumption, for behind the facade of success, problems were rapidly coming to a head. By July 1943, the number of aircraft devoted to air defence had grown to about 800 day- and 600 night-fighters, with inevitable effects on Luftwaffe strength elsewhere. More importantly, many of the best fighter pilots were involved in the battle to protect German cities and, as their losses mounted, the Luftwaffe was denuded of its best men. Although some were lost at night, hit by machine-gun fire from

Below: A Messerschmitt Bf 110G-4, originally of Nachtjagdgeschwader 4, photographed post-war at RAF Farnborough. It is equipped with a FuG 218 Neptun radar, the aerials of which can be seen in the nose.

Left: A Luftwaffe non-commissioned officer displays his bomb-disposal skills, Berlin, 1943. RAF bombing raids on the German capital often left unexploded ordnance that needed clearing – a dangerous and laborious business. Here, the NCO appears to be dealing with a small incendiary device.

Right: Members of the Luftschutz (Air Raid Services) distribute gas masks and show small children how to wear them. The photograph probably dates from 1939 or 1940, when the threat of gas attack seemed real. Similar scenes were played out in Britain, although in the event neither side used chemical weapons. High explosive and incendiary weapons were a far greater threat to the average German citizen.

Below: Luftwaffe mechanics service and repair the Daimler-Benz DB 601E-1 12-cylinder liquid-cooled inverted-vee engine belonging to the Messerschmitt Bf-109F fighter in the background. Regular servicing was vital if the Luftwaffe was to maintain effectiveness in the skies over Germany.

the bombers or occasionally by shells from their own anti-aircraft batteries, most of the casualties were imposed by the Americans during daylight hours. The reason was simple: in the aftermath of the heavy B-17 losses against Regensburg and Schweinfurt – losses which could, of course, be replaced much more quickly than those suffered by the Germans – American commanders had concentrated on the development of escort fighters, capable of accompanying the bombers deep into Germany and taking on the

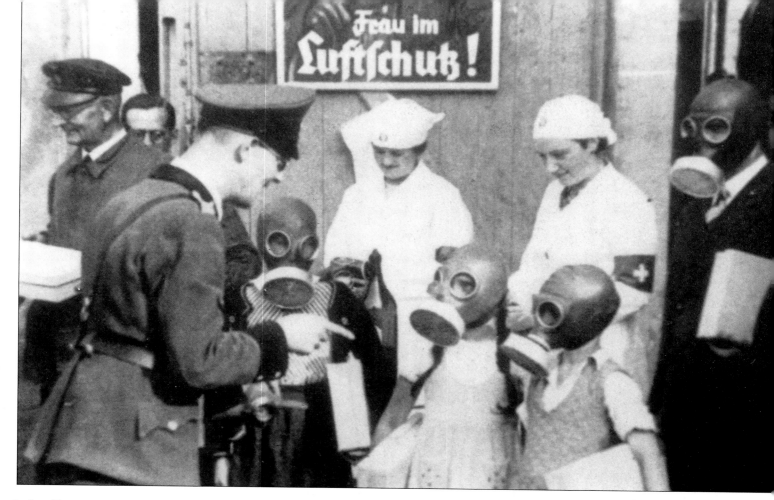

Luftwaffe in air-to-air combat. Initially, they had improved the range of existing fighters, such as the Republic P-47 Thunderbolt, by attaching drop-tanks for extra fuel, but in the autumn of 1943 they introduced the North American P-51D Mustang.

The mighty Mustang

This remarkable aircraft, created by marrying a Mustang airframe to a Rolls Royce engine, not only had the range to escort the bombers to Berlin and beyond, but also proved more than a match for the Bf 109 and Fw 190. Before the appearance of the American escort fighters, the Luftwaffe had devoted resources towards increasing the hitting-power of its single-engined fighters, so they could more easily destroy the US bombers. However, this meant extra weight, which put the German pilots at a disadvantage if engaging American fighters in dogfights. A sort of answer was to divide fighters between 'heavy' and 'light' fighter groups. The heavy groups were equipped with Bf 109s and Fw 190s fitted with heavy batteries of cannon for attacking bombers, while the light groups operated lightly armed Bf 109s to tackle the escorts. Problems arose when the American fighters were in such force that they were able to cut through the light groups to wreak havoc upon the 'heavies'.

The Luftwaffe was given a short respite in April 1944, as the Allied bomber fleets downgraded their attacks on Germany in order to concentrate against more tactical targets in direct support of the forthcoming D-Day landings. However, there was no doubting that the tables had been turned.

The results were catastrophic for the Luftwaffe. General Adolf Galland, a noted 'ace' and now *Inspekteur der Jagdflieger* (Inspector of Fighters), reported that 'between January and April 1944 our day-fighter arm lost more than 1000 pilots. They included our best *staffel*, *gruppe* and *geschwader* commanders'. With the Allied air forces enjoying air superiority, at least by day, and the Luftwaffe seriously overstretched, Galland was more than justified in concluding that 'the time has come when our force is within sight of collapse'. That would come as the Soviets continued to thrust westwards and the Anglo-Americans prepared for the long-awaited invasion of Western Europe.

A force bled white

Despite incredible bravery and improvisation, leading to one of the most effective (albeit short-lived) air-defence campaigns of the war, the Luftwaffe was reaching the end of its capability. Once it could no longer control the skies over Germany, its enemies were free to concentrate their massive resources on the destruction of key industries and lines of supply. And these industries included factories that were producing fighters. A further problem was that the Messerschmitt Me 262, the only aircraft capable of evading the American escorts, was being produced as a fighter-bomber under Hitler's express orders. This delayed production of this excellent jet aircraft by several crucial months. From now on, Göring's men would be fighting to survive rather than to win, against an enemy who had unlimited resources. It was a far cry from the heady days of the Blitzkrieg.

CHAPTER 9

RED STORM

In 1944-45 the Luftwaffe maintained a substantial presence on the Eastern Front, but the Russians launched a series of massive offensives that smashed the Germans on the ground and in the air.

Left: A leutnant, serving in a Luftwaffe Field Division, watches as Junkers Ju 87 Stukas fly over towards Soviet lines, 1944. He is probably in radio contact with the pilots.

Above: Soviet Ilyushin Il-2 Type 3M ground-attack aircraft over the Eastern Front, 1944. Purpose-built for close support of ground forces, it had specially armoured engine and cockpit areas.

By 1 January 1944, the Luftwaffe had a front-line strength of just over 5500 combat aircraft, about 1700 of which were deployed on the Eastern Front. In themselves, these were not unreasonable figures – they represented a statistical improvement on a year before – but they disguised a host of serious weaknesses.

Because of decisions made as early as 1941, aircraft production had tended to concentrate on proven designs, merely updating and uprating them as time went on, neglecting the full development of fresh ideas. Some new machines were becoming available, not least the long-awaited He 177 and Junkers Ju 188 bombers, though

Above: A Gotha Go 242A assault and transport glider lifts off under tow, winter 1943-44. The aircraft is dropping its wheels to make it lighter and to improve aerodynamic shape.

Below: A Junkers Ju 52 transport is prepared for take-off on an airfield on the Eastern Front, winter 1944-45. The pipes into the port nacelle carry hot air to warm the engine.

Above: A Messerschmitt Me 231A-1 heavy transport glider is pulled into the air by a pair of Heinkel He 111H-6 bombers joined together and given a fifth engine. Known as the Heinkel-Zwilling, this rather unconventional combination was first used to deliver supplies to the men of the trapped Sixth Army in Stalingrad in early 1943.

Below: A clearer view of the unusual Heinkel-Zwilling, showing the engine layout and enormous wingspan of 35m (116ft). The two He 111H-6 fuselages were attached by means of a new centre-wing section, strengthened to take a fifth engine. The aircraft – now known officially as the He 111Z – was flown from the port cockpit.

there were never enough of them to have an appreciable effect on combat power. Frontline squadrons depended on stalwarts such as the Bf 109 and Ju 88, while the Fw 190 had proved an adaptable and, at times, quite formidable, fighter, but when it is realised that the Bf 110 and even the Ju 87 were still being modified and deployed, despite their painfully apparent obsolescence, the nature of the problems facing the Luftwaffe may be appreciated.

Fatal flaws in the aircraft industry

But those problems went much deeper. On the one hand, Allied bombing raids were beginning to bite by early 1944, hitting key components of the aircraft industry, including engine plants and fuel supplies; on the other, all Allied powers were now producing superior aircraft designs, which left the Luftwaffe struggling to keep up. In the East, the Soviets had not only deployed specific ground-attack machines, such as the Ilyushin Il-2 and Petlyakov Pe-2, but were also well on the way to developing and fielding the next generation of fast interceptor fighters, such as the Lavochkin La-7 and Yakovlev Yak-3, both of which were more than capable of matching the latest modifications of the Bf 109 or Fw 190. Moreover, by early 1944 the Soviet Air Force was outnumbering the Luftwaffe by a factor approaching six to one, giving it the luxury of gaining air superiority wherever and whenever it was needed. Although 1700 combat aircraft might have looked good on paper, the Luftwaffe had a front of nearly 3200km (2000 miles) to cover and just could not do so with any hopes of lasting success.

Opposite above: Luftwaffe crew members pause to synchronise their watches before boarding their bomber. The three on the right are wearing the correct life jacket for crews of bombers, transports and flying boats, but the man on the left has managed to acquire an example of that issued to fighter pilots.

Opposite below: A Junkers Ju 52 is prepared for a day's work by ground crew, who are removing the tarpaulins from cockpit and engines. The wheel fairings, with their painted lines, suggest that this is a civilian airliner, possibly belonging to Lufthansa.

Right: With bow doors wide open, a Messerschmitt Me 323D-1 Gigant *(Giant)* six-engined transport waits to be off-loaded, 1944. Capable of carrying up to 18,180kg (40,000lb) of supplies, it was extremely vulnerable in the air.

Below: A massive Messerschmitt Me 231A-1 glider being towed aloft by a trio of Bf 110C fighters, 1943. This combination, known as Troika-Schlepp, was not a great success, chiefly because of problems coordinating the towing aircraft. By 1943, the Bf 110s had been replaced by the five-engined Heinkel He 111Z (see page 131).

Above: A Junkers Ju 88C pressed into service as a cargo-carrier, Eastern Front, 1944. The bomb appears to be a 1000-pounder, and behind it are crates of supplies for aerial delivery.

Below: An unusual sight by 1944-45: a flight of Junkers Ju 88s flies into the attack. Such a group of flying machines would be an inviting sight for Soviet interceptor aircraft.

This had been apparent in the campaigns of late 1943, when attacks had occurred primarily in the south, for the Soviets had always ensured that air superiority was attained, at least on a localised basis. What was emerging was a distinctive Soviet war-fighting philosophy, based in part on lessons drawn from the experiences of 1941-43, and in part on theories of 'deep battle' first propounded in the inter-war period. Enormous emphasis was laid on *maskirovka* – deception designed to enhance surprise by tricking the enemy into believing that an attack was about to happen elsewhere – and the air force played its part in this by concentrating in one place then attacking elsewhere, something that could only be done with large numbers of aircraft available. Once surprise had been achieved, avenues of advance would be carved out by overwhelming mechanised force, supported by massed air capability, which would observe the enemy's deployments, act as 'flying artillery' to blast a way forward, cut off enemy lines of supply and communication and, if necessary, resupply ground elements from the air. The overall aim was to advance into the depth of the enemy, disrupting his ability to respond and shattering his will to fight. If this could be done simultaneously along vast portions of the frontline, so much the better, as the Germans would be stretched and weakened.

Soviet force levels were such that they could start to do this in early 1944, mounting offensives from Leningrad in the north to

Above: By 1944, German engineers were experimenting with high-altitude bombers in an attempt to avoid Allied air defences. Here, a Junkers Ju 88S is shown, fitted with nitrous-oxide injected BMW 801G-2 engines. The experiment was a success.

Below: One of the more unusual Luftwaffe designs of the war was the Blohm und Voss Bv 141 tactical reconnaissance and army cooperation aircraft. The aircraft, powered by a single engine, never entered squadron service.

Above: A Junkers Ju 87 banks to starboard over the River Dnieper. Its bomb racks are empty, implying a successful mission, but its days as an effective aircraft are numbered. As soon as the Soviets gain air superiority, the Stuka will be a doomed weapon.

Opposite below: Romanian troops, fighting on the side of the Germans, watch as a number of Junkers Ju 87 Stukas peel away, having carried out dive-bombing attacks on nearby Soviet positions, 1944. The troops are well dug-in, clearly expecting a ground assault – the Stukas have given them a respite.

the Crimea in the south. With less than 350 fighters available all along the Eastern Front, there was little the Luftwaffe could do to withstand the pressure, particularly as any attempt to concentrate resources in one sector were doomed when attacks began elsewhere. Some local successes were enjoyed – in mid-January, for example, the Luftwaffe managed to deliver over 2032 tonnes (2000 tons) of supplies to forces trapped in the Cherkassy 'pocket', and two months later a similar operation enabled the First Panzer Army to survive encirclement – but the costs were heavy. Over 650 transports were lost during the first five months of 1944, at a time when production of such aircraft had taken second place to fighters and bombers. Luftwaffe strength was being eroded steadily, not least in terms of trained pilots and crews.

A hare-brained scheme

The situation was not helped by a sudden decision, made by Hitler and Göring in November 1943, to mount a strategic bombing campaign against Soviet industry. Göring's subsequent directive was crystal clear: 'I intend to unite the majority of the heavy bomber units assigned in the East ... [to be given] the mission of conducting air attacks against the Russian armaments industry

with a view to destroying Soviet material resources ... before they can be put to use at the front.' However, this was something for which the Luftwaffe was neither trained nor equipped, as was to become painfully apparent.

Eight bomber *gruppen* (about 250 aircraft, mostly He 111s) were withdrawn from frontline service, and preparations made to hit factories chiefly around Gorky. However, by the time the force was ready in late March 1944, Soviet advances had pushed the bomber bases so far west that the He 111s were effectively out of range of their targets. With the longer-range He 177s and Ju 188s unavailable in sufficient numbers, there was nothing that could be done to carry out Göring's wishes. The bombers soon found that demands for their services from hard-pressed ground units took precedence, particularly as the whole experiment coincided with the withdrawal of fighter (and fighter-bomber) squadrons to defend the German homeland. All that was achieved was that for about four months the bombers were not available to bolster defences in the East.

Göring rebuilds his shattered squadrons

Fortunately for the Germans, the Eastern Front stabilised somewhat in April 1944, as the Soviets prepared their next series of offensives. Göring took the opportunity to rebuild his squadrons, taking advantage of a simultaneous lull in Anglo-American bombing raids as the Western allies shifted air support to the projected amphibious assault on 'Fortress Europe'. The results were impressive: by 1 June the three *luftflotten* in the East were fielding a total of nearly 2000 combat aircraft, the majority of which were ground-attack and bomber designs. The emphasis lay with *Luftflotte 4* in the south. Here, 850 aircraft covered the approaches to the vitally important Romanian oilfields, where the main weight of the next Soviet assault was expected to fall, although the central region, defended by *Luftflotte 6*, was not neglected, with over 770 machines available. The real weakness lay in the north, where *Luftflotte 1* had fewer than 400 aircraft, none of which were bombers and only 70 were ground-attack designs – inadequate numbers to stop the Russians. Given recent losses in all theatres, however, this was a remarkable achievement.

But it was not enough. The Soviets, for good reason, dubbed the campaigning season of 1944 the 'Year of Ten Victories', indicating just how flexible and wide-ranging they had become. Thus, when the expected offensive began in early June 1944, it did not materialise in the south immediately, but was presaged by an attack in the far north against Finland, where Luftwaffe defences were at their weakest. German and Finnish air capability was swept aside by sheer weight of numbers, forcing the Luftwaffe to send reinforcements from *Luftflotte 6*. This was exactly what the Soviets wanted, for on 23 June they opened their main attack – Operation 'Bagration' – on the central front, where they had massed over 6000 combat aircraft. As Army Group Centre fought for its very existence, Hitler authorised the withdrawal of aircraft from other theatres – 40 fighters from the defence of Germany, 85 from Italy and 40 from *Luftflotte 3* in Western Europe – but to little avail. Within less than three weeks, the Soviets had punched an enormous hole in the German defences, allowing them to advance almost 800km (500 miles) by the end of July, to the borders of East Prussia. Army Group Centre ceased to exist, along with nearly 400 Luftwaffe aircraft.

Nor was this the end of the nightmare, for the long-awaited assault in the south began on 20 August, at a time when most Germans had assumed the area to be secure. By then, *Luftflotte 4*

had been reduced to less than 200 combat aircraft as reinforcements had been rushed farther north, and when this coincided with the sudden collapse of Romania, the Soviets were able to advance with comparative ease. By 31 August, most of Romania had been occupied; by mid-September Bulgaria had switched sides, declaring war on Germany, and Soviet troops had entered northern Yugoslavia and eastern Hungary. Luftwaffe squadrons continued to fly, but they were finding it increasingly difficult to guarantee the existence of secure bases and were encountering overwhelming Soviet air strength. As the year came to an end, the remnants of the Luftwaffe in the East were being squeezed back into Germany to join their comrades now fighting the Western allies. It was a hopeless task.

Defeat, retreat and destruction

The lull which occurred on the Eastern Front as the Soviets built up their forces for the next offensive did not last long. Even if it had, the Luftwaffe was rapidly approaching a situation in which it could no longer be revitalised. Over 13,000 aircraft had been lost in all theatres during the course of 1944, and production had suffered under the relentless weight of enemy bombing attacks, falling to little over 3000 machines in December. Moreover, as the Soviets advanced from the east they overran Luftwaffe training bases, established there to avoid attack from the Western allies, and their withdrawal into Germany not only led to hopeless congestion but also disrupted the replacement of lost aircrews. Finally, as predominantly American bombers deliberately targeted oil facilities, fuel shortages curtailed air operations and reduced the levels of air support available to frontline ground units.

Opposite above: The crew of a Soviet Ilyushin Il-2 hurry through the cold of their airfield, discussing tactics and their recent experiences of battle, February 1944.

Opposite below: Soviet Ilyushin Il-4 bombers, fitted with 45-36-N low-level release torpedoes, fly towards their targets, 1944. With a maximum speed of 416kmph (260mph) and a range of 3776km (2360 miles), the Il-4 was a capable machine.

Right: Soviet Ilyushin Il-2 Type 3M aircraft seek out German panzer formations, 1944. Operating in a 'Circle of Death', whereby each aircraft attacked in turn until ammunition ran out, the Il-2s were rightly feared by enemy troops.

Below: The price of German failure in the East: the graves of fallen soldiers stand in front of a ruined Russian village, 1944.

The next Soviet attack began on 12 January 1945 and was stunning in both its scope and impact. *Maskirovka* had led German ground commanders to expect the full weight of the offensive to fall around Warsaw; in reality it came farther south, bursting out of bridgeheads on the west bank of the Vistula River at Sandomierz and Magneszew. *Luftflotte 6*, facing the central front, had more than 1000 aircraft available and enjoyed the advantage of operating from concrete runways inside Germany, but the Soviets, true to form, had amassed overwhelming numbers of aircraft to support the breakthrough sectors. By 19 January, Soviet troops had breached the eastern borders of Germany; by the end

of the month, they had reached the River Oder, less than 80km (50 miles) from Berlin, creating bridgeheads on the west bank from which they could assault the capital. Additional aircraft were scraped together from all theatres and hastily committed to try to stem the flow. Altogether, nearly 800 machines were found, but their crews were largely inexperienced and the Soviets were able to wreak havoc. Although they halted their attacks in February, having advanced nearly 800km (500 miles) and stretched their logistic chain to the limit, the end was clearly in sight.

One result was that, as the Soviets resumed their advances all along the Eastern Front, they encountered little opposition from a

Above: A Junkers Ju 87G-1, fitted with two underwing 37mm Flak 18 cannon, stands at dispersal on a German airfield, 1944. The cannon were designed as anti-tank weapons, but made an already slow aircraft even less manoeuvrable.

Below: Men of a German armoured formation, moving over open terrain on the Eastern Front, wave to acknowledge the arrival of a Junkers Ju 87 Stuka. Despite its obsolescence, the Stuka continued to be deployed right up to the end of the war.

defeated and shattered Luftwaffe. In the south, for example, *Luftflotte 4* tried to defend an area from the Adriatic Sea to the Carpathian Mountains with a force of little more than 500 aircraft, most of which were wasted when Hitler ordered a counterattack to relieve the siege of a German garrison in Budapest. The Soviets immediately responded, ejecting the Germans from Hungary by the end of March and taking Vienna on 13 April. By then, *Luftflotte 4* had ceased to exist. Similar attacks in the centre, aimed at Berlin, began in late April. Despite bitter fighting on the ground – by the fall of the German capital in early May, the Soviets had suffered over 100,000 casualties – the Luftwaffe had virtually no discernible impact. There was literally nothing left to give.

The Eastern Front in retrospect

Viewed in retrospect, the failure of the Luftwaffe in the East is not difficult to explain. From the start of 'Barbarossa' in June 1941, Hitler had expected his air force to do too much, covering an enormous frontage with inadequate resources. The Luftwaffe had been designed and trained for short, sharp campaigns, and despite the outstanding achievements of 1941, once the war in the East entered a second year, it would have taken a radical shift in priorities and industrial procedures to transform the force into one that was able to cope with a lengthy conflict. Faced with a Soviet Air Force which used the time to develop and grow, the numerical odds were soon stacked against the Luftwaffe, while the steady

Above: The aftermath of a successful Stuka tank-busting attack: a Soviet T-34/85 lies wrecked by cannon fire. Such damage could be easily absorbed by the Soviets, whose tank factories were working at full capacity by 1944.

Below: Hans-Ulrich Rudel (centre), the most highly decorated Stuka pilot of World War II. Here he wears the Knight's Cross with Golden Oakleaves and Diamonds, of which he was the only recipient. He survived the war, having flown over 2000 sorties.

Above: *Field Marshal Maximilian, Baron von Weichs (centre) returns from a personal reconnaissance mission in a Fieseler Fi 156* Storch *light aircraft in the background, probably during his time as Commander of Army Group B on the Eastern Front, 1943. By then, the Fi 156 was a vulnerable machine.*

Left: *A Focke-Wulf Fw 190A-4/U3 of* Schlachtgruppe 1 *on the Eastern Front, early 1945. The addition of bombs to the Fw 190 created an effective fighter-bomber.*

Opposite above: Oberst *Hermann Graf (second from left) with fellow pilots of* Jagdgeschwader 52 *on the Eastern Front. Graf was the first Luftwaffe fighter pilot to reach a total of 202 aerial victories, of which 200 were against the Soviets.*

improvements to Soviets technology, coming at a time when the Germans were having to go for larger numbers of already existing designs in a vain bid to maintain viability, merely made things worse. In such circumstances, air superiority was impossible to retain and, once that could no longer be guaranteed, ground forces were left unprotected and vulnerable to defeat.

But the Soviets were not the only threat. While German forces battled for survival in the East, the Western Allies used their air strength not only to wear down the Luftwaffe still more but also to devastate its infrastructure. The oil industry and aircraft-production plants were included on the list of targets for the vast fleets of Allied bombers. The end in the West was just as traumatic and decisive as that in the East.

CHAPTER 10

WESTERN ONSLAUGHT

The Luftwaffe was hard pressed to even compete with Allied airpower over Italy and northwest Europe, and what little strength it had was thrown away in Hitler's last gamble in the West – the Ardennes Offensive.

Left: Civilians watch as an air armada carrying paratroopers on Operation 'Varsity' – the crossing of the Rhine – passes overhead.

Above: RAF armourers prepare to load air-to-ground rockets onto a Hawker Typhoon 1b of No 609 Squadron, France, August 1944.

German fears of a ground war on more than one front had become a reality as early as September 1943, when Anglo-American forces invaded Italy, landing across the Straits of

Messina from Sicily and launching an amphibious attack at Salerno, just to the south of Naples. Adolf Hitler's decision to fight for control of the Italian peninsula was unavoidable – if he

Above: *Messerschmitt Bf 110Cs of* Zerstörergeschwader 26 *on a forward airstrip in Sicily, July 1943. By this stage in the war,* *the Luftwaffe is struggling to maintain air superiority, though enemy air attack is clearly not expected in this case.*

had merely allowed the Allies to occupy the country his entire southern flank would have been dangerously exposed – but it quickly became apparent that he did not have the resources needed to do the job. Although land battles in late 1943 and early 1944 delayed the Allied advance, bogging it down in the mountainous approaches to Cassino and Rome, the Luftwaffe was not strong enough to make any decisive impact. At the beginning of 1944 *Luftflotte 2*, responsible for the Italian theatre, had no more than 370 aircraft available, of which less than 100 were bombers or ground-attack machines.

Poor showing in Italy

Reinforcements were found after the Allies tried to break the deadlock around Cassino by landing farther north, at Anzio (22 January 1944), but the numbers were still inadequate. By late January, 140 bombers had been brought in from Greece, France and Germany, including Do 217s and He 177s equipped with Hs 293 and *Fritz X* radio-controlled bombs. Their novelty value did have a temporary effect, sinking a number of Allied warships and merchantmen. A serious shortage of fighters, however, meant that the Luftwaffe never gained air superiority, and the Allies were able to destroy many of the bombers before they could find suitable targets. By the same token, the despatch of 50 fighters from Western Europe in early March was insufficient to enable ground forces to execute successful counterattacks against the new beachhead or in the area of Cassino. By late March 1944, it was obvious that airpower was being wasted and a number of squadrons were redeployed. Thereafter, the Luftwaffe played little part in the Italian campaign, leaving ground units to use their ingenuity and terrain advantages in order to survive. It was not what the Wehrmacht had been trained to expect.

By then, it was apparent that Allied landings on the northern coast of occupied Europe would not be long delayed. On 1 April, substantial elements of the Anglo-American bomber fleet were shifted from strategic attacks to ones that were designed to support

Right: The aftermath of an Allied air attack on a German airfield near Trapani in Sicily on 26 July 1943.

an amphibious assault. Though none of the German commanders could be sure where or when the landings would take place, Allied preparations gradually wore down defences throughout the theatre. One of the prerequisites for Allied success was air superiority, to protect both the invasion fleet and the forces once ashore. *Luftflotte 3*, covering France and the Low Countries, was reinforced, partly at the cost of the Italian theatre but also because some squadrons protecting the homeland could be diverted now that Allied bombers were otherwise occupied, but as in Italy and the East, there were never enough aircraft to go around. Thus, though the highly experienced close-support formations of *Fliegerkorps II* were transferred from northern Italy to *Luftflotte 3* in February 1944 and, a month later, the anti-shipping experts of *Fliegerkorps X* joined them, Anglo-American air superiority was already such that they could only assume the defensive, waiting for the inevitable attack.

Renewed attacks on Britain

This was something that neither Hitler nor Göring was prepared to do. Just as on the Eastern Front, they insisted on an air offensive to try to disrupt enemy preparations. As early as 3 December 1943, Göring issued a directive ordering renewed bombing attacks on Britain. A total of 525 bombers were scraped together, but the raids, known to the British public as the 'Baby Blitz', were disastrous for the Luftwaffe. Between 21 January and the end of May 1944, 29 raids were carried out, during which nearly 3048 tonnes (3000 tons) of bombs were dropped, but at a cost of 329 precious aircraft. Some of the attacks were targeted against ports in southern England in hopes of disrupting the invasion build-up, but they had little impact against well coordinated defences, and actually prevented proper air reconnaissance from taking place. By early June, *Luftflotte 3* had just over 800 aircraft available and had no clear idea of where the invasion would come. By then, the Allies had amassed more than 7000 aircraft, enough to ensure that attacks could be carried out all along the disputed coastline, disguising the true intention of an attack in Normandy. And ensuring total Allied air superiority.

Top left: A Focke-Wulf Fw 190A, captured intact by the Allies after being abandoned on an airfield near Naples, September 1943. Note the bomb under the fuselage and the empty racks under the wing. If it could avoid enemy air defences, the Fw 190A was an effective fighter-bomber.

Above: A Heinkel He 177A-5/R2 six-seat heavy bomber, reconnaissance and anti-shipping aircraft in 1943. This particular machine has underwing racks for radio-controlled bombs such as the Fritz-X *or Hs 293. He 177s were used to bomb Britain in the so-called 'Baby Blitz' of early 1944.*

Right: A Dornier Do 217K-2 night-bomber, photographed in December 1942. This version of the Do 217 differed from earlier models in terms of its redesigned forward fuselage, extending the glazed panels to the nose, and its ability to carry and launch radio-controlled bombs. It saw service in Kampfgeschwader 100.

Above: *The effects of Allied air superiority: a German train, camouflaged in a vain attempt to escape attention, stands wrecked in the rail yards at Münster, April 1945. Allied interdiction of enemy supply lines had largely succeeded by this stage in the war, disrupting the movement of troops and supplies.*

Left: *Allied air-to-ground rockets head towards their targets, Normandy, July 1944. The ability to hit enemy road and rail communications played a key role in the breakout battles in August.*

Opposite below: *British intelligence officers examine the remains of a Messerschmitt Bf 109G, shot down near Tilly-sur-Seulles in Normandy, July 1944. Luftwaffe activity in northern France was curtailed by fuel shortages and overwhelming Allied superiority.*

The results were inevitable. On 6 June 1944, the Anglo-Americans used their air superiority to drop paratroopers on the flanks of the assault area, to observe enemy positions on the coast, to lend close support to troops as they went ashore and, most significantly, to interdict German lines of supply and communication. Altogether, the Allies flew more than 14,000 air sorties on D-Day itself, to which *Luftflotte 3* could respond with a mere 319. Most of the attacking troops saw no sign of the Luftwaffe during the day of the invasion or, indeed, during the succeeding weeks. It was a comprehensive display of aerial power which Göring could not hope to match.

But it would be wrong to assume that the Luftwaffe did nothing. As soon as the invasion occurred, reinforcements were despatched – some 300 fighters and 120 bombers by mid-June – and attempts were made to carry out attacks, not least against the Allied naval and transport fleet concentrated offshore. Sea mines were dropped, usually at night, and high-level bombing raids were executed, although the impact was small. By August, when the Allies finally broke out of the close country around Caen in Normandy, there was nothing to prevent their rapid advance to liberate Paris and sweep on into Belgium and towards the German frontier. In the process, German troops learnt what it was like to suffer constant air attention: those trapped in the 'Falaise Pocket' in late August came under sustained attack from rocket-firing Typhoon and Thunderbolt fighter-bombers, losing their equipment and combat cohesion and suffering heavy casualties. The Luftwaffe could do nothing to help.

Nor could it prevent a resumption of the Anglo-American strategic bombing campaign. Raids on key German targets had not ceased entirely during the Allied build-up to D-Day, but once the troops were safely ashore and the breakout from the beachhead had been achieved, the bomber fleets were free to turn their full attention to the German homeland, attacking both by day and by night. German air defences were still theoretically formidable – by 1 October 1944, for example, the number of night-fighters available to combat the RAF's heavy bombers had risen to 830 – but the practical problems of operating the Luftwaffe effectively were legion. During daylight hours, American escort fighters – now capable of flying the length and breadth of Germany with fuel to spare for air-to-air combat – protected the B-17s and B-24s. At night, new British jamming techniques rendered the SN-2 *Lichtenstein* radars of German fighters inoperable, leaving frustrated pilots to scour the darkness for elusive targets. Even when the Luftwaffe managed to gain a technological advantage, as with the deployment of jet- and rocket-powered aircraft (see Chapter 11), the lack of fuel and of pilot experience left the Allies relatively secure. In the end, it was Luftwaffe-manned anti-aircraft guns as much as fighters that imposed losses on the enemy air forces.

German cities and industry bombed

The Allies responded to their achievement of air superiority over Germany in two ways, both of which hastened the destruction of the Nazi regime. The Americans, always more in favour of concentrating against key components of the enemy's war machine than his civilian workforce, sought out facilities connected to oil, transportation and the air industry, the destruction of which did nothing to improve matters for the Luftwaffe. By comparison, the RAF sent increasingly strong forces against cities and the industrial complexes within them, culminating (with some American day-

Above: As the war in northwest Europe draws to a close, the remains of the Luftwaffe are either destroyed or captured by Allied troops. This is a hanger at Wunstorf near Hanover.

Below: Once the Luftwaffe has been swept from the skies, the bomber fleets enjoy free rein. This photograph of B-17s of the US 8th Army Air Force gives a good impression of Allied airpower.

Top right: An RAF reconnaissance photograph, taken in early October 1944, shows a relatively undamaged portion of the Krupps armaments factory in Essen. A major raid, involving 1055 bombers, was mounted on the night of 23/24 October.

Below right: A post-raid reconnaissance photograph shows damage inflicted on the Krupps works at Essen on 23/24 October 1944. Buildings have been devastated, but Bomber Command carried out two follow-up raids to ensure complete disruption.

light help) in the controversial bombing of Dresden on 13/14 February 1945. The creation of a 'firestorm', similar to that which had devastated Hamburg 18 months earlier, led to the deaths of at least 50,000 civilians. RAF Bomber Command, having committed 796 Lancasters and nine Mosquitoes to the attack, lost just six aircraft to enemy defences. The whole of Germany lay vulnerable, bereft of the one instrument that might have protected it: an effective air force.

It was not just the practical problems of fuel shortages, pilot inexperience and enemy superiority that destroyed the Luftwaffe in the West. Hitler's strategic decisions also played an important part, wasting the assets that were still available. His plans for 'reprisal' attacks on Britain at a time when Allied air superiority was such that the attempt was doomed to failure, caused irreplaceable losses to the Luftwaffe's bomber arm, but the real damage came (eventually) at the very beginning of 1945. As the Western Allies advanced towards Germany in the autumn of 1944, Hitler perceived a potential weakness in their deployment, with the Anglo-Canadian thrust into the Low Countries veering away from the American spearhead towards the German frontier. The area in-between included the heavily wooded Ardennes, scene of the panzer breakthrough in 1940. Hitler convinced himself that this success could be repeated, despite differences in enemy capability and time of year. In great secrecy, he prepared an armoured attack that would thrust through the Ardennes and split the Anglo-Canadians from the Americans. Even if the Western Allies did not collapse, time would be gained for a German concentration of resources against the Soviets in the East.

The Ardennes Offensive

It was an over-ambitious plan in every way. The commitment of Germany's last major reserves, both on the ground and in the air, meant that failure would be catastrophic, with little remaining to prevent defeat. Nevertheless, the secret deployment of nearly 30 divisions, 10 of them armoured, was supported by an impressive total of 2460 aircraft, the bulk of which were fighters, tasked with the destruction of Allied airbases in accordance with Blitzkrieg tradition. As the panzers pushed through to the Meuse River, the plan was for the Anglo-American tactical air forces to be so badly hit that they would be incapable of interfering, at least during the early, crucial, stages of the offensive. Codenamed *Bodenplatte*

Above: *Gunther Bahr (centre) poses with his crew in front of their Messerschmitt Bf 110G night-fighter, 1945. Bahr has just been told that he has been awarded the Knight's Cross, but he has not yet received the medal.*

Below: *Two night-fighter pilots celebrate having received their Knight's Crosses, 28 January 1945. On the left is Stabsfeldwebel Ludwig Bellof; on the right Stabsfeldwebel Leopold Hackl. Both served with* Nachtjagdgeschwader 3.

('Ground Plate'), it was all set to begin on 16 December 1944, the opening of what the Americans would later call the 'Battle of the Bulge'. It was to be Hitler's last gamble in the West.

The weather negates airpower

Bodenplatte did not take place as planned, principally because of the weather. One of the reasons for choosing such a late date for the attack was that Allied airpower would be grounded by fog or snow, but if that was the case on enemy airfields, then it was only logical that it would be the same on their German equivalents. For most of the first week of the 'Battle of the Bulge', neither side could deploy its airpower effectively; something that was far more of a loss to the Germans than it was to the Allies. Despite quite deep advances into the Ardennes by panzer task forces, some of which reached to within 16km (10 miles) of the Meuse, the Americans were strong enough to absorb the blow and push in seemingly limitless reinforcements to contain (and squeeze) the 'bulge'. Moreover, once the weather cleared, Allied air advantages were apparent. Fighter-bombers swooped down to hit panzers that were desperately short of fuel, supplies were dropped to sustain American paratroopers besieged in Bastogne, and bombers started to sever the links between frontline German formations and what little they still had by way of support. Luftwaffe aircraft that appeared were promptly shot down by defending fighters or anti-aircraft units.

Above: General Adolf Galland salutes as a wreath is laid to commemorate Oberst *Walter Oesau, killed in a dogfight with US fighters over the Eifel region of Germany on 11 May 1944.*

Below: Oberst *Walter Oesau, photographed in early 1944. He was the third Luftwaffe fighter pilot to achieve the magic figure of 100 aerial kills; he scored another 23 before he was killed.*

Top left: *Messerschmitt Bf 110D long-range fighters of Zerstörergeschwader 1 over the Eastern Front, 1944. Note the elaborately painted representation of a wasp on the nose of the lead aircraft – ZG1 was known as the Wespen Geschwader and pilots took pride in advertising the fact. By 1944, this was perhaps not advisable.*

Middle left: *A rather unusual Junkers Ju 88G night-fighter, equipped with Lichtenstein radar but powered by what appear to be supercharged engines driving four-bladed propellers.*

Above: *General view of a crowded Heinkel factory. Such German manufacturing potential had been largely destroyed by Allied bombers by 1945.*

Above: *A Heinkel He 219A Uhu (Owl), equipped with SN-2 Lichtenstein and C-1 Lichtenstein radar antennae. The He 219 was the heaviest of the German night-fighters, but development was slow and the first examples did not enter squadron service until mid-1943. Thereafter, they exacted a steady toll on British bombers but were too few in number to make a difference.*

But Hitler remained convinced that an all-out air effort was still viable. As a result, at 0900 hours on 1 January 1945 a total of nearly 800 Bf 109s and Fw 190s, equipped as fighter-bombers, took to the skies, aiming to destroy the Allied air forces in northwest Europe. It was a forlorn hope, for though some minor successes were achieved through surprise – an attack against the airbase at Eindhoven, for example, inflicted significant damage on two Canadian Typhoon squadrons – the Luftwaffe's losses were crippling. By the end of the day about 200 of the attackers had been shot down, depriving the Germans of pilots they could ill afford to lose. By comparison, the Allied loss of 144 aircraft, many of them unmanned on the ground, was easy to replace from reserve stocks.

With the failure of *Bodenplatte*, the Luftwaffe in the West was finished as an effective fighting force. Crippling fuel shortages

were such that entire formations of aircraft were grounded, while many of the new machines still being produced (largely in factories that had been dispersed away from the cities to avoid Allied bombing) could not be delivered because of enemy air attacks on transportation systems. Even if the new aircraft had reached the frontline, the chances of them being properly crewed were minimal, the training organisation having virtually collapsed. In such circumstances, there was little to stop Allied aircraft from roaming at will over a rapidly shrinking Reich. What did remain, however, was a variety of 'wonder weapons', the story of which is one of missed opportunities and false hopes, epitomising many of the problems which bedevilled the whole of the Luftwaffe throughout its brief existence. That story needs to be told before any final judgements can be made.

CHAPTER 11

TOO LITTLE, TOO LATE

The Luftwaffe produced a number of technologically advanced fighter and bomber designs, which could have made a difference to the outcome of the war, but delays and political interference negated their effectiveness.

Left: A spectacular display of anti-aircraft tracer fire lights up the sky over southern England as defences concentrate against incoming V1 'flying bombs', late 1944.

Above: A bizarre Luftwaffe design was the Mistel 1 *– a Junkers Ju 88 airframe, its cockpit replaced by a hollow-charge explosive device, which was carried to its target by a Bf 109F.*

More than 100,000 Luftwaffe aircraft were lost between 1939 and 1945, while 320,000 of its personnel were killed and 230,000 seriously injured. Not only had air superiority been lost in all theatres by 1945, but many of the aircraft then remaining in frontline squadrons were outclassed by their Allied counterparts. Incapable of defending the skies above Germany, Luftwaffe pilots could only watch as Allied bombers wreaked havoc; unable to provide close support to battered ground forces, those same

Above: An impressive line-up of Messerschmitt Me 262A single-seat twin-jet fighters, possibly of **Kommando Nowotny,** *early 1945. The primary task of these aircraft was to intercept and destroy Allied bombers. They marked a new era in air combat.*

Below: Oberst *(Colonel) Gunther 'Franzl' Lutzow, holder of the Knight's Cross with Oakleaves and Swords. Killed in April 1945, he was credited with 108 aerial victories. He was described by Adolf Galland as 'the outstanding leader in the Luftwaffe'.*

pilots could do nothing to prevent the advance of enemy armies from both East and West. It was a far cry from the victorious campaigns of 1939-41.

The reasons for this dramatic decline in combat power are obvious in retrospect. There is no doubt that the Luftwaffe of 1939 was hiding behind a facade of political bluster, and was not nearly as effective as it appeared to be. The rapid expansion of 1935-39 was unbalanced, lacking depth in terms of funding and development, so that aircraft designs in service over Poland remained in frontline units throughout the war, being modified but not replaced. A new generation of fighters and bombers, promised in the late 1930s and essential if the Germans were to retain their technological edge, never materialised in the numbers expected, reflecting an air industry that found it increasingly difficult to cope with the demands of conflict. As losses mounted and Blitzkrieg campaigns gave way to the hard slog of total war, new developments were often cancelled or postponed so that proven designs could be produced in sufficient numbers to satisfy frontline demands.

Of equal importance was the nature of those demands. The pre-war Luftwaffe was designed essentially to support the army,

Above: The lack of unit markings suggests that this is a pre-delivery example of the Messerschmitt Me 262 jet fighter. The slightly swept-back wings and nacelles for the two Junkers Jumo 004B axial-flow turbojets are shown to advantage.

Below: Hauptmann *(Captain) Walter 'Nowi' Nowotny, a* Luftwaffe *'ace' with 258 aerial kills to his credit, all but three of them on the Eastern Front. He was killed in a dogfight with USAAF P-51 Mustangs over Germany.*

chiefly by gaining air superiority over the battle area and then disrupting enemy countermoves. Yet as the war went on, these tasks were extended to include strategic bombing of enemy cities, close support of forces on the ground as they engaged the enemy, resupply of encircled armies, and defence of airspace over Germany itself. In all cases, existing aircraft designs were ill-suited, creating more pressures on manufacturers as modifications had to be introduced swiftly. Even then, there were limits, for the German economy, so hastily revitalised by Hitler in the mid-1930s, creaked beneath the strain of prolonged conflict. Aircraft continued to be manufactured right up to the end of the war – indeed, under the leadership of Albert Speer as Minister of Armaments and Munitions after 1942, production levels rose to new heights – but Anglo-American bombing disrupted the means of delivering them to frontline squadrons and destroyed remaining stocks of fuel. At the same time, the Americans, Soviets and British either created or expanded war economies to cope, producing aircraft that were not only technologically superior to many of the German designs but were also available in far larger numbers. Moreover, the Allies provided trained manpower to fly the aircraft in combat, something the Luftwaffe was incapable of doing by 1945, its training

Above: One of the 'A' series prototypes of the Arado Ar 234 Blitz jet-powered bomber at the moment of take-off, April 1944. The undercarriage trolley has just been disengaged.

Below: An Arado Ar 234B abandoned on a German airfield. The fixed undercarriage is an improvement on the 'A' series. The engines are Junkers Jumo 004B Orkan axial-flow turbojets.

Above: *The Ar 234 was the subject of a number of experiments during its short life-span. Here, the Ar 234 V13 variant mounts four BMW 003A-1 turbojets, mounted in pairs on each wing, in an effort to improve power and speed.*

Below: *Hanna Reitsch (centre), reputedly the only female civilian to be awarded the Iron Cross during the war, discusses the finer points of gliding. On 26 April 1945, Reitsch flew General Ritter von Greim, who replaced Göring, into Berlin.*

squadrons having been decimated in battle. In the end, the Luftwaffe was out-fought and out-produced, facing threats and realities that neither Hitler nor Göring fully appreciated.

The deadly Swallow

Yet the fact remains that, in certain respects, the Luftwaffe retained a promise of technological advantage which, if it had been exploited, might have made an appreciable difference. On 25 July 1944, for example, a British pilot reported having encountered an aircraft of incredible speed high over southern Germany. What he had seen was a Messerschmitt Me 262 turbojet, known to its crews as the *Schwalbe* (Swallow). Capable of a top speed of 864kmph (540mph) at 6096m (20,000ft), an initial rate of climb of nearly 1219m (4000ft) a second and a radius of action of more than 480km (300 miles), it represented a quantum leap in air technology, outpacing and out-flying most existing piston-engined designs. The aircraft had its origins as far back as 1938, though the prototype did not actually fly until March 1942, there being no urgency at a time when most Germans were still confident of victory. Problems occurred with the jet engines, and the

Below: A rare photograph of the Heinkel He 178, the world's first aircraft to fly purely by turbojet power. It took to the air on 27 August 1939, 20 months before the British-built Gloster E.28/39. The He 178 prototype was destroyed when the Berlin Air Museum was bombed in 1943.

Above: *A Heinkel He 162 single-seat jet fighter takes to the air. This aircraft, captured in May 1945, was shipped to the United States for flight evaluation, where this photograph was taken. The nose markings suggest that it served in* Jagdgeschwader 1.

Below: *Pilots compare notes as their Heinkel He 162s stand idle for lack of fuel, April 1945. This photograph was proably taken at Leck, where* Jagdgeschwader 1 *was concentrated. The He 162s never fired a shot in anger.*

aircraft was clearly too delicate for front-line duties at that stage, but some Luftwaffe commanders, notably Adolf Galland (who flew the prototype), appreciated its revolutionary nature. On 25 May 1943, Galland urged Göring to concentrate resources on the Me 262, with the aim of producing at least 1000 aircraft a month by 1944. If this had been acted upon, the war in the air could have taken a different course (though it is worth bearing in mind that the British were also developing jet fighters, the first of which, the Gloster Meteor, entered squadron service in late July 1944).

Delays in the Me 262 programme

As it was, the opportunity offered to Germany was wasted. Because of frontline demands, production of the Bf 109 and Fw 190 took priority, with more confidence being expressed in the latter's piston-engined successor, the Ta 152, than the new-fangled (and as yet unproven) turbojet. In addition, in June 1943 Hitler insisted on the Me 262 being produced as a fighter-bomber rather than a conventional fighter, and though the impact of this decision should not be exaggerated – the main problems lay in production, not deployment – the enforced addition of a 250kg (550lb) bomb reduced speed and spoilt the aerodynamic qualities of the aircraft. Allied bombing of key factories, especially those engaged in the production of the Junkers jet engines, did nothing to help matters, with the result that relatively few Me 262s saw

Above: The Dornier Do 335 V1 prototype, which flew for the first time on 26 October 1943. Known officially as the Pfeil *(Arrow), it was soon nicknamed the* Ameisenbär *(Ant Eater) because of its odd shape.*

frontline service before the end of the war. By April 1945, despite Hitler's reversal of his earlier decision, only about 200 of the jet fighters were available for combat. They had been used principally against B-17s in daylight, and US airmen had been suitably impressed, but serviceability and sortie levels had remained low, reducing overall impact. Also, inadequate pilot training and an inability to concentrate massed formations of Me 262s meant that the jets could be countered, even using piston-engined Mustangs flown by experienced pilots. By the end of the war it was estimated that Me 262s had destroyed about 150 enemy aircraft in combat, yet had suffered 100 losses themselves. It was a poor record.

Other revolutionary designs suffered a similar fate. The Arado Ar 234 *Blitz* (Lightning), for example, was the world's first operational jet bomber, capable of carrying a bomb load of 1500kg (3300lb) over a radius of 560km (350 miles) at a top speed of 736kmph (460mph), but when it was first developed in 1941 there seemed no reason to accelerate production. By the time it was needed, factories were unavailable and other demands were taking priority. The first production models were not introduced

into service until June 1944; by April 1945, only 38 of the twin-jet machines were with frontline units. Most were being used for reconnaissance, as they were the only Luftwaffe aircraft able to penetrate Allied air defences with any degree of impunity.

Given the prevarications and delays, it is therefore surprising to discover that a third jet aircraft, the Heinkel He 162 *Salamander*, was rushed into production in late 1944 on the personal insistence of Hitler and Göring. Known unofficially as the *Volksjäger* (People's Fighter), it was designed, flown and tested in the unprecedented period of 90 days, with orders that it should go into full production and be piloted by Hitler Youth boys. With the emphasis on ease of manufacture – the He 162 was made of light alloys and plywood – the aircraft had some potential: it could reach a top speed of over 896kmph (560mph) and was armed with lethal 20mm cannon. But, once again, it was a case of too little, too late: by the end of the war only 50 of the machines had been delivered to frontline units and none had seen action. If they had, their record would probably have been similar to that of the Japanese *kamikaze* (suicide) aircraft of the Pacific War.

Nor were jets the only development. In piston-engined terms, the Dornier Do 335 *Pfeil* (Arrow) was unconventional (it was driven by two propellers, one at the front of the aircraft and one at the back), but when first flown in October 1943, showed significant promise, reaching a top speed of 758kmph (474mph)

Above: The interior of the Dornier factory at Oberpfaffenhofen as it appeared when US forces captured the facility in May 1945. The aircraft under construction in the foreground is a Do 335 A-12 tandem two-seat dual-control trainer, only two of which were ever completed.

Below: Another shot of the Dornier Do 335 V1 prototype, this time during flight trials at Oberpfaffenhofen in late 1943. Despite its odd design, it proved to be a reasonably easy aircraft to fly, with better acceleration and turning circle than had been expected. The external oil cooler intake was later deleted.

Above: *Messerschmitt Me 163B-1a Komet rocket-powered fighters stand at dispersal on a German airfield, 1945. The tarpaulin covers suggest that operational flying is unlikely.*

Below: *A standard production Messerschmitt Me 163B-1a, 1945. It was an impressive machine, but its unstable fuel and short flying duration seriously undermined its effectiveness.*

while armed with a 30mm cannon and two 15mm machine guns. Despite its odd configuration, this could have been a useful machine. Unfortunately for the Luftwaffe, the project was cancelled in late 1944. Even more futuristic was the Messerschmitt Me 163 *Komet* (Comet), a rocket-powered aircraft which held the record as the fastest aircraft of the war years. Fuelled by an extremely unstable mix of propellants, it proved to be something of a death-trap for its pilots, who not only faced the awesome experience of travelling at nearly 960kmph (600mph), but also watched as the aircraft jettisoned its wheels on take-off, depending on small skids on which to land after a sortie lasting less than seven minutes. Me 163s did enter squadron service, claiming the destruction of nine enemy bombers, but the fact that this cost them 14 of their own aircraft to achieve meant the cost-effectiveness of the rocket fighter was hard to justify. A further design, the Bachem BA 349 *Natter* (Adder), was even more terrifying: it was to be launched vertically to the altitude of enemy bombers, whereupon the pilot would fire air-to-air rockets before bailing out. Fortunately for all concerned, the *Natter* never got beyond trial launches.

More success was enjoyed by another of the 'wonder weapons', the Fieseler Fi 103: a pilotless aircraft usually known as the V1

(*Vergeltungswaffe 1* or Vengeance Weapon No 1). It made its first test flight as early as December 1942 and offered a number of advantages. Being pilotless, it saved manpower and training time, while its relatively cheap construction, using pressed steel rather than increasingly scarce aluminium, promised mass production at little cost to the German war economy. The Argus pulse-jet engine was complex and fraught with problems, but once they had been sorted out, the 'flying bomb' was found to have an effective range of about 240km (150 miles). This opened up the possibility of bombarding Britain from special launch rails in northern France, each V1 carrying a warhead of 850kg (1870lb) which, it was predicted, could be delivered with some accuracy. Once a V1 was launched, its engine would take it to its operating altitude of 914m (3000ft) and propel it at 640kmph (400mph) for about 30 minutes; the fuel would then run out, upon which the aircraft would fall to the ground and explode.

Below: A close-up of a Mistel 2 *combination, captured by US troops in May 1945. The Focke-Wulf Fw 190F-8 on top was designed to jettison the Junkers Ju 88G-1, loaded with high explosives, once the target had been reached.*

Responsibility for deploying the V1 was given to the Luftwaffe flak arm, and a special regiment (*Flakregiment 155(W)*) was created in late 1943. At the same time, 96 concrete launch sites were constructed in northern France, with an intention of initiating attacks on London in December 1943. But such elaborate preparations were impossible to hide from the Allies, who received information from aerial photo-reconnaissance and French Resistance workers. The launch sites proved easy to spot and, in a series of air attacks, the majority were destroyed. Earlier raids on the development complex at Peenemunde on the Baltic coast, the most effective of which occurred on the night of 17/18 August 1943, further delayed V1 deployment. It was not until June 1944 that enough of the flying bombs were stockpiled for a sustained campaign, using much simpler (and camouflaged) launch ramps.

The V1 campaign

The V1 assault began on the night of 12/13 June, only six days after the Allied landings in Normandy. It was not a success: instead of a mass attack from all launch sites simultaneously, 10 V1s took to the air, of which only one made it through to London, the rest succumbing to a variety of mechanical problems. But these were merely teething troubles. When the campaign began in earnest three days later, it proved possible to fire up to 190 aircraft a day. By 1 September, when advancing Allied troops began to overrun the launch sites, more than 8600 flying bombs had been aimed at southern England. The campaign was then taken over by specially adapted He 111s, each capable of air-launching a single V1. They continued operating until January 1945, by which time longer-range V1s were being fired from sites in the Netherlands.

The V1 balance sheet

The last effective launch against England occurred on 30 March 1945. By then, about 10,500 V1s had been used, the bulk of them fired from ground ramps in France or Holland. Of that total, 7488 actually crossed the English coast and 2450 impacted, within the city limits of London (2419), on Southampton/Portsmouth (30) and on Manchester (one). The rest either failed mechanically in flight or were intercepted and destroyed by Allied defences. Anti-aircraft fire was found to be effective once the operating altitude of

Below: An early model of the Henschel Hs 293 radio-controlled bomb is shown slung beneath a Heinkel He 111 bomber, 1942. This a is a cut-down version of the Hs 293, implying that it is being used for glide-flight trials.

Above: *A Blohm und Voss Bv 143 rocket-powered air-delivered torpedo is wheeled out for attachment to an He 111. The Bv 143 was designed to be released at an altitude and range impossible for conventional torpedoes.*

Below: *A Bv 143 aerial torpedo is released during trials in 1943. The arm hanging down is a 'feeler': once the torpedo glided down to 2m (6.5ft) above the surface of the sea, the arm touched the waves and triggered the rocket motor.*

the V1 was worked out, and fast fighters (including Meteors) were capable of shooting the missiles down or even, in extreme cases, flying alongside, carefully placing a wingtip under that of the flying bomb and then flipping it over. Nevertheless, by the end of March 1945 some 6184 civilians had been killed and 17,981 injured by the flying bombs. However, like the air campaign against Britain waged by the Luftwaffe in 1940, the V1s did not affect the morale of the population.

Other 'Vengeance Weapons', notably the V2 surface-to-surface missile operated by the German Army, also contributed to the campaign. If weapons such as these had been available in sufficient numbers earlier in the war and coordinated with conventional bombing raids, their impact might have been significant. As it was, their development had been left too late and their attacks initiated at a time when Allied air superiority left them and their launch sites vulnerable. By then, the Luftwaffe was already a broken force.

Below: A dramatic photograph, taken on 15 June 1944 looking over the Piccadilly area of London, shows a Fieseler Fi 103 or V1 'flying bomb' diving towards the ground. Its fuel has run dry, leaving it to fall like a brick; its 850kg (1870lb) warhead will explode on impact.

Right: An A4 surface-to-surface rocket, more familiarly known as the V2, is put on show in London after the war, letting the people of the British capital see what it was that bombarded their city in 1944-45. Altogether, 1054 V2s, all launched by the German Army, fell on Britain.

Below right: Hermann Göring, photographed after his capture by Allied troops in May 1945. He is still wearing his medals, including (around his neck) the Pour le Mérite *and Grand Cross of the Knight's Cross, the latter the only one ever awarded.*

FURTHER READING

David Baker, *Adolf Galland. The Authorised Biography*
(Windrow & Greene, London, 1996)

Werner Baumbach, *Broken Swastika. The Defeat of the Luftwaffe*
(Robert Hale, London, 1960)

Matthew Cooper, *The German Air Force 1933-1945: An Anatomy of Failure*
(Jane's, London, 1981)

Brian Ford, *German Secret Weapons: Blueprint for Mars*
(Pan/Ballantine, London, 1972)

William Green, *Warplanes of the Third Reich*
(Macdonald and Jane's, London, 1970)

E R Hooton, *Phoenix Triumphant: The Rise and Rise of the Luftwaffe*
(Arms and Armour Press, London, 1994)

David Irving, *The Rise and Fall of the Luftwaffe. The Life of Luftwaffe Marshal Erhard Milch*
(Weidenfeld & Nicolson, London, 1974)

Heinz Knoke, *I Flew For The Führer*
(Evans Brothers, London, 1953)

R J Overy, *The Air War 1939-1945*
(Europa Publications, London, 1980)

Alfred Price, *Luftwaffe: Birth, Life and Death of an Air Force*
(Pan/Ballantine, London, 1973)

Hans Ulrich Rudel, *Stuka Pilot*
(Ballantine Books, New York, 1958)